Catalogue of British and European Prehistoric Metalwork in Birmingham City Museums

Philip J. Watson

BAR British Series 233

1993

Published in 2019 by
BAR Publishing, Oxford

BAR British Series 233

Watson Philip J. 1993
Catalogue of British and European Prehistoric Metalwork in Birmingham City Museums

ISBN 9780860547587 paperback
ISBN 9781407318592 e-book

DOI https://doi.org/10.30861/9780860547587

A catalogue record for this book is available from the British Library

This book is available at www.barpublishing.com

BAR Publishing is the trading name of British Archaeological Reports (Oxford) Ltd.
British Archaeological Reports was first incorporated in 1974 to publish the BAR
Series, International and British. In 1992 Hadrian Books Ltd became part of the BAR
group. This volume was originally published by Tempvs Reparatvm in conjunction
with British Archaeological Reports (Oxford) Ltd / Hadrian Books Ltd, the Series
principal publisher, in 1993. This present volume is published by BAR Publishing,
2019.

BAR

PUBLISHING

BAR titles are available from:

BAR Publishing
122 Banbury Rd, Oxford, OX2 7BP, UK
EMAIL   info@barpublishing.com
PHONE   +44 (0)1865 310431
FAX   +44 (0)1865 316916
www.barpublishing.com

INTRODUCTION

The purpose of this catalogue is simple: to make the collections of prehistoric European metalwork in Birmingham Museums known to a wider audience. All too often museum collections remain hidden away in store rooms where they are almost as lost to scholarship as if they had never been preserved. With the ever increasing pressures of time and cost on research projects few scholars are able to visit and browse through such collections. Therefore if this catalogue enables researchers to determine whether Birmingham contains anything of relevance to their studies without recourse to futile visits or lengthy correspondence it will have served its purpose. Although some of the British material is already published it is scattered through various county journals and other publications and none of the foreign material has been published previously nor included in the relevant editions of *PBF*.

No attempt has been made to treat each object exhaustively and descriptions have been kept to a minimum as have lengthy discussions on date, typology and provenance; most of the pieces fall into well known categories for which typological and chronological frameworks already exist. Moreover, the scope of the collections puts any meaningful synthesis of their wider context out of the question in a work of this size and nature. Several indices and concordances have been provided to facilitate access to the material.

Inevitably decisions had to be made as to what it was pertinent to include and these were taken on the basis of the nature of the Birmingham collections. Generally speaking all pre-Roman metalwork from "Barbarian" Europe has been included. The majority of Italic and Etruscan items, notably figurines, mirrors, fibulae, so-called bit-spacers and a small group of finds from Cumae, have been excluded as these are better placed amongst the Mediterranean collections. However, pre-Roman fibulae with a known provenance outside Italy have been included as have a few Roman pieces from Swiss Lakes assemblages. Cypriot pieces have been omitted as these have already been published collectively (Peltenburg 1981). Likewise the Celtic coins have been separately published (Gunstone 1971, Symons 1988) and, besides, form the subject of a distinct specialist discipline. Finally, all material which is on loan to the department and therefore not part of our permanent collections is excluded.

As always with a museum catalogue there are more people deserving of acknowledgement than can be individually mentioned. Obviously a debt of gratitude is owed to previous curators and scholars who have worked on the collections and recorded their comments and opinions about particular items. I must thank my colleagues at Birmingham, David Symons and Jane Peirson Jones, for their advice and helpful comments throughout the preparation of this catalogue. Special thanks are due to Carol Selby who typed up the manuscript and masterminded the layout and design. Finally most grateful thanks must go to the several friends, students and volunteers who, over a period of years, have produced the drawings without which this catalogue would have little value. They are:

Lynne Barrett: ills. 367, 369, 370, 428, 429

Gail Falkingham: ills. 142, 195–197, 202–216, 218–220, 224, 225, 228–236, 239, 242, 243

Sue Gill: ills. 143–186, 188–190

Zoe Ibbotson: ills. 200, 253, 255, 257–263, 290–322, 326, 349–351, 366, 368, 373, 393–397, 414–418, 423, 424, 435, 452, 453, 470, 474, 479–483, 486–488, 494, 495, 497–501, 505–507, 509, 510

Chris Kirby: ills. 33–35, 37, 38, 40–48, 50, 52–55, 57, 68, 69, 109–118, 120–123, 125, 126, 128, 130–135, 137, 138, 221, 222, 226, 227, 240, 241, 514–525, 533–538, 540–551, 553

Aileen McAuly: ills. 331–348, 352–365, 371, 372, 374–392, 398–413, 419–422, 425–427, 430–433, 496

Megan Mentz: ills. 191, 266–269, 271–283

Dave Trueman: ills. 119, 124, 129

Any illustrations not listed above are by the author.

HISTORY OF COLLECTIONS

The collection of prehistoric metalwork in Birmingham Museum has grown unevenly but steadily over the 107 years since the museum's founding through a combination of small private donations of chance finds, selective purchases and acquisition of larger existing collections. Growth was at first slow with less than fifty pieces being acquired in the first 65 years. However, following the creation of a separate department of archaeology in 1951 (hitherto archaeological objects had been curated either by the Natural History department or the Applied Arts department, depending on their nature) a more active collecting policy was pursued beginning with a quantity of Swiss Lakes material from one of the Lake Neuchatel sites purchased from Worcester Museum. This was followed in 1957 by a collection including British and Irish bronzes purchased from the Birmingham Archaeological Society. All of these pieces had been bequeathed to the Society in 1935 on the death of T.G. Barnett, a well known local antiquarian and member of several archaeological societies; he had assisted on local excavations and was a keen collector, notably of watches, silver plate, and antiquities.[1]

A decade later, after a few small, though in some instances significant, purchases the department acquired a large quantity of prehistoric material bought from the Salisbury and South Wiltshire Museum. This came from the collection of William Blackmore and comprised over 1300 prehistoric artefacts, mainly stone implements from France, the Swiss Lakes and Denmark but also including bone work from France and Swiss Lakes sites and about seventy bronzes, predominantly from France. Another large collection which contained prehistoric bronzes was purchased from the Birmingham University Medical School in 1973. This was a very mixed collection of both archaeological and ethnographic material from all over the world.

The size of the prehistoric metalwork collection was almost doubled in 1983 with the purchase of another large early collection of over 800 prehistoric items, on this occasion from Mrs. S. Pitt-Rivers. This contained predominantly neolithic and bronze age material from the Swiss Lakes of Neuchatel and Bienne and the Lac du Bourget in France. There was also some material from Denmark and a few miscellaneous pieces from elsewhere. The Pitt-Rivers Swiss lake material was probably all collected in the late 1800's as several pieces have labels recording previous collectors of that period. Most frequently mentioned is Lawrence, presumably Geoffrey F. Lawrence of Wandsworth, who sold a collection of Swiss lake material to Liverpool Museum in 1899 (Caunce 1982, 3) and from who Birmingham University Medical School appear to have acquired an Irish piece (no. 130 in the catalogue below). A handful of pieces were formerly in the Roots collection, sold at Christies on 20th April 1891 and at least one is ex Bryce-Wright (Stevens sale, 23rd March 1888).

---

[1] See obituaries in *Transactions of the Birmingham and Warwickshire Archaeological Society* LIX (1935), 170; *Birmingham Mail* 8th May 1935; *Birmingham Post* 6th May 1935. The prehistoric gold items in Barnett's collection (nos. 101–108) below were bequeathed directly to the museum in 1935 as part of his spoon and jewellery collection.

CATALOGUE

NOTE ON LAYOUT OF ENTRIES

The catalogue is divided by country beginning with Britain, followed by Ireland and then the rest of Europe arranged alphabetically except for Denmark and Sweden which are put together under Scandinavia. Within each country entries are arranged by object type following the sequence hoards, tools, weapons, ornament. The format for each entry is as follows:

1. *Catalogue number:* which also refers to illustration number. Note however that some minor objects have not been illustrated whilst some of the more complex pieces appear as photographic plates rather than as line drawings. The illustrations are at 1:2 unless otherwise stated.

2. *Description:* as mentioned in the introduction these have been kept deliberately brief. It should be assumed that all objects are made of copper or copper alloy unless the material is specifically given.

3. *Provenance:* arranged in descending hierarchy i.e. county or region, site, national grid reference. Where known details of the circumstances of discovery are also given.

4. *Dimensions:* given in centimetres. The following abbreviations are used:

   av.   average
   Di.   diameter
   H.   height
   L.   length
   max.   maximum
   Th.   thickness
   W.   width
   wt.   weight

5. *Acquisition details:* acquisition method, source, date, previous collection number and pedigree where known.

6. *Bibliography:* references are given only for the object in question, not comparanda.

7. *Accession number:* (duplicate accession numbers are given in brackets).

8. *Comments and observations:* again these have been kept to a minimum.

ENGLAND [1—108]

1—10
Founder's hoard.
Surrey, Carshalton Park, TQ 281640. Found in March 1905 during building operations.
Presented by Mrs. G.A. Clayton 1953 ex collection H.C. Collyer.
Collyer 1908, 208; Phillips 1967, 15; Phillips 1968, 130—132.

1
Centre winged axe with side loop and notch in butt for hafting peg. One wing damaged and one entirely broken away.
L. 14.0 cm., blade W. 3.5 cm.
1953A850.3

2
Fragment of centre winged axe. Blade, butt and wings all broken off. Remains of side loop.
extant L. 8.4 cm.
1953A850.1

3
Fragment of centre winged axe. Blade, butt and wings all broken away.
extant L. 7.2 cm.
1953A850.4

4
Plain socketed axe with single mouth moulding; mouth and blade damaged.
L. 9.0 cm., max. W. 4.2 cm.
1953A850.5

5
Socketed axe with double mouth moulding; mouth damaged on one corner. One short haft rib preserved, other obscured by corrosion. South Eastern type.
L. 8.8 cm., max. W. 4.7 cm.
1953A850.6

6
Socketed axe with double mouth moulding; blade damaged. Two haft ribs in socket, one on each face. South Eastern type.
L. 10.4 cm., max. W. 5.1 cm.
1953A850.7

7
Socketed axe with double mouth moulding and four raised pellets below preserved on one face only; obscured by corrosion on other. Blade missing and some damage to mouth. South Eastern type.
extant L. 7.7 cm.
1953A850.8

8
Socketed axe with triple mouth moulding. Large elongated blow hole in one side below loop; blade damaged. South Eastern type.
L. 10.4 cm., blade W. 3.7 cm.
1953A850.9

9
Fragment of heavy socketed axe; lower part only. Blade not sharpened. Breton type.
extant L. 6.5 cm., max. W. 4.1 cm.
1953A850.2

10
Socketed axe with widely spaced double mouth moulding. Long haft ribs in socket.
L. 9.1 cm., max. W. 4.0 cm.
1953A850.10

11—19
Founder's hoard.
Norfolk, Gorleston-on-Sea II. Discovered whilst laying pipes.
Purchased 1966.
Christies 25/10/1966 lot 7.

11
Three-ribbed socketed axe with double mouth moulding.
L. 8.9 cm., max. W. 5.4 cm.
1966A668.3

12
Socketed axe with double mouth moulding. Two
tapering haft ribs in socket, one on each face.
South Eastern type.
L. 9.7 cm., max. W. 4.3 cm.
1966A668.2

13
Socketed axe with double mouth moulding. South
Eastern type.
L. 9.8 cm., max. W. 4.0 cm.
1966A668.1

14
Socketed axe with double mouth moulding and
highly expanded blade. Two haft ribs in socket.
L. 6.6 cm., max. W. 4.2 cm.
1966A668.4

15
Fragment of sword preserving hilt and top of blade
only. Blade of lozenge section with central rib
extending onto hilt as far as first rivet hole.
Marked ricasso. Three rivet holes in each shoulder
and three more in hilt plate. Hilt ribbed. Type
Ewart Park.
extant L. 15.1 cm.
Colquhoun and Burgess 1988 no. 398.
1966A668.6

16
Fragment of sword; tip of blade only.
extant L. 7.4 cm.
Colquhoun and Burgess 1988, pl. 168J.
1966A668.7

17
Pegged socketed spearhead; tip missing.
extant L. 10.4 cm.
1966A668.8

18
Pegged socketed spearhead; tip missing and socket
squashed.
extant L. 8.4 cm.
1966A668.9

19
Casting jet from mouth of funnel with one runner
and trace of second. Possibly from casting of a
socketed spearhead.
L. 2.3 cm., di. 3.1 cm.
1966A668.5

20-21
Founder's hoard.
Middlesex, Hanwell. Exact circumstances of find
not recorded. Found before 1904.
Purchased Birmingham University Medical School
1973.
Windle 1904, 93-94 gives analysis of ingots as
0.863% S, 0.079% Pb and 0.038% Fe; Sn, Sb, Zn and
Ni were tested for but not found.

20
Fragment of socketed axe with double mouth
moulding; blade missing. Two long haft ribs in
socket.
extant L. 4.9 cm.
1973A326.1

21
Thirteen fragments from circular plano-convex
copper ingots.
Diameters can be reconstructed at between 13-20
cm.
1973A316 to 1973A325, 1973A326.2 to 1973A326.4

22-29
Founder's hoard.
Southern England, no provenance; possibly East
Anglia.
Purchased R.T. Clough 1958.

22
Plain socketed axe with double mouth moulding.
L. 10.3 cm., max. W. 4.7 cm.
1958A243.1

23
Plain socketed axe with double mouth moulding.
L. 9.7 cm., max. W. 4.3 cm.
1958A243.2

24
Plain socketed axe with double mouth moulding.
L. 10.1 cm., max. W. 5.0 cm.
1958A243.3

25
Plain socketed axe with double mouth moulding.
Blow hole low down on one face.
L. 10.7 cm., max. W. 4.3 cm.
1958A243.4

26
Upper part only of plain socketed axe with double
mouth moulding. Blow hole through one side near
loop.
extant L. 5.9 cm.
1958A243.8

27
Fragment of plain heavy socketed axe with double
mouth moulding. Blade broken off. There is a
fragment of another implement? wedged in the
misshapen socket.
extant L. 6.4 cm.
1958A243.7

28
Faceted socketed axe with slight raised band at
level of top of loop beyond which the mouth flares
outwards. Four long haft ribs in socket - one on
each face and one on each side.
L. 10.4 cm., max. W. 5.4 cm.
1958A243.5

29
Fragment from centre of blade of a hollow
sectioned sword.
extant L. 6.5 cm., max. W. 4.7 cm.
1958A243.6

30-32
Part of hoard.
Northamptonshire, near Oundle; dug up by a farmer
in a field. There were originally about 80 pieces in
all in an earthenware jar.
Presented by Col. A. Constantine in 1957.
Moore 1977, 209.

30
Plain, faceted socketed axe with no mouth
moulding. Two short haft ribs in socket. Blow hole
in one face at height of loop.
L. 7.2 cm., blade W. 3.6 cm.
1965A501 (1948A4.4).

31
Faceted socketed axe with slight raised band at
height of top of loop beyond which the socket
flares outwards.
L. 8.8 cm., blade W. 4.3 cm.
1968A288 (1948A4.6).

32
Plain socketed axe with no mouth moulding. Poorly
cast with part of mouth missing and cracks in
blade. Short but prominent haft rib in socket on
one face; other face damaged.
L. 7.8 cm., blade W. 4.6 cm.
1965A502 (1948A4.5).

33
Cast flanged axe; butt possibly originally longer.
Berkshire, Maidenhead.
L. 10.6 cm., max. W. 4.5 cm.
Purchased Sandy 1948.
1966A32.

34
Haft flanged axe with low stop ridge. Cole's class
II - possibly Irish in origin.
Staffordshire, Wolverhampton; found in October
1969 whilst excavating a pipe trench in grounds of
Parkfield Infant School. SO 921963.
L. 13.1 cm., max. W. 4.7 cm.
Purchased W.T. Bull 1969.
Gunstone 1972, 48 no. 3; Rowlands 1976, no. 277;
Vine 1982, no. 799.
1969A1059.

35
Early shield pattern palstave with fairly high
flanges. Highly expanded blade. Swallow hole at
base of stop ridge on one side.
Norfolk, Norwich.
L. 15.5 cm., max. W. 6.5 cm.
Purchased Sandy 1948.
Rowlands 1976, no. 776.
1966A36.

36
Early shield pattern palstave. Swallow hole below
stop ridge. Burgess group I.
Warwickshire, Curdworth, SP167925.
L. 17.5 cm., max. W. 8.1 cm.
Acquired from Rev. Duffy.
Mitchell 1923, 76; Rowlands 1976, no. 1025; Vine
1982, no. 750.
1949A18.

37
Shield pattern palstave. Burgess group I.
Warwickshire, Birmingham; found in garden of 337
Haunch Lane, Kings Heath in 1969 whilst
gardening. SP 085802.
L. 16.6 cm., max. W. 6.3 cm.
Presented by Mrs E.E. Cosnett 1969.
Sunday Mercury, 14/12/1969, 11; Thomas, 1970, 180;
Rowlands 1976, no. 1027; Vine 1982, no. 751 (note
wrong acc. no.).
1969A989.

38
Shield pattern palstave. Burgess group I.
Warwickshire, Coventry; possibly near Pageant
House in Cox Street.
L. 14.5 cm., max. W. 5.2 cm.
Presented John Staunton 1875, ex William Staunton.
Rowlands 1976, no. 1024; Chatwin 1922, 172 no. 9.
1885A1499 (1948A4.1).
Apparently it was used in the Coventry pageants as
a prop.

39
Shield pattern palstave. Burgess group I.
Warwickshire, Meriden. SP 261843. Metal detected
1978.
L. 15.7 cm., blade W. 5.8 cm., wt. 407 gm.
Presented Mrs. H. Dymond 1983.
Vine 1982, no. 753; Watson 1984, no. 2.
1985A32.

40
Badly damaged palstave with traces of shield
pattern. Blade, butt and flanges all damaged; badly
pitted where corrosion has been cleaned off.
Swallow hole in septum near stop ridge on one
side.
Staffordshire, Wednesfield; found in garden of 21,
Mercer Grove before 1961.
SJ 95090148.
extant L. 11.2 cm., extant max. W. 3.6 cm.
Presented Mrs. E. Griffiths 1961.
Gunstone 1972, 50 no. 5; Vine 1982, no. 777.
1971A17.

41
Low-flanged palstave with central rib; unlooped.
Flanges extend beyond stop ridge onto blade.
Swallow hole at base of stop ridge on one side.
Burgess group II (early).
Norfolk, Norwich.
L. 16.2 cm., max. W. 6.9 cm.
Purchased Sandy 1948.
Rowlands 1976, no. 255 (note wrong acc. no.).
1966A35.

42
Unlooped low-flanged palstave with central rib.
Burgess group II.
Warwickshire, Birmingham; found in garden of 186
Flaxley Rd., Stechford c. 1939 during construction
of an air raid shelter. SO 135876.
L. 16.1 cm., max. W. 6.5 cm.
Presented C.L. Schlamm 1954.
Gunstone 1965, 94—95; Rowlands 1976, no. 1028;
Vine 1982, no. 763.
1954A621.

43
Unlooped palstave with central rib. Burgess group
II.
Worcestershire, Beoley, near Icknield Street;
discovered whilst road making in 1933.
L. 16.1 cm., max. W. 7.1 cm.
Presented by J.R. Ratcliffe 1933.
Smith 1957, 18; Rowlands 1976, no. 1064.
1933A24 (1948A4.2).

44
Unlooped low-flanged palstave with projecting stop
ridge and indistinct Y-shaped rib. Butt broken.
Casting seams not trimmed and blade not
sharpened. Burgess group II.

England, no provenance.
extant L. 9.9 cm., max. W. 4.2 cm.
Acquisition details unknown.
1962A398.

45
Unlooped low-flanged palstave with slight central
rib. Casting flashes not trimmed. Burgess group II?
Britain, no provenance.
L. 16.7 cm., max. W. 6.6 cm.
Purchased Birmingham University Medical School
1973.
1973A301.

46
Low-flanged looped palstave with trident pattern
rib. Loop broken. Burgess late group IIIa.
Staffordshire, Wolverhampton area, SO9198; found
about 1907.
L. 13.5 cm., max. W. 6.0 cm.
Presented R.W. Crossland 1947.
Rowlands 1976, no. 914; Vine 1982, no. 786.
1948A4.9.
Apparently the brother of the donor obtained the
piece from a brass founder in the Wolverhampton
area who had discovered the piece originally,
analyzed it and cast copies (six or seven) of it.
Subsequently the casts and the copies became
mixed up.

47
Low-flanged looped palstave with central rib; loop
broken. Swallow hole in stop ridge. Burgess group
IIIa.
Warwickshire, Barton Green near Kenilworth,
SP2675; discovered whilst laying foundations
shortly before 1914.
L. 15.1 cm., max. W. 5.7 cm., wt. 316.9 gm.
Presented Mrs. W.A. Beamish 1946.
Humphreys 1944, 141–142; Rowlands 1976, no. 1026.
1946A66 (1948A4.3).
Analysis: Cu 81.0%, Sn 11.0%, Pb 0.9%, Zn 2.7%, Fe
and Al present but not determined, Sb, As, P not
assayed.

48
Low-flanged looped palstave with central rib.
Burgess group IIIa.
Staffordshire, Middleton, SP189980; found in a field
during ploughing c.1958 and used for a while as a
paint scraper.
L. 16.7 cm., max. W. 7.0 cm.
Presented R. Moulton 1971.
Vine 1982, no. 783.
1972A131.

49
Low-flanged looped palstave with central rib and
broad expanded blade; loop broken. Burgess group
IIIa.
Worcestershire, near Berry Mound. Found in 1979.
SP 09917780.
L. 16.0 cm., max. W. 6.3 cm.
Purchased Fox & Co., Yeovil 1983.
Watson 1984, 3 no.3.
1983A113.

50
Low-flanged looped palstave with central rib and
crinoline outline; blade damaged. Three short ribs
in hafting slot on each side running from stop
ridge. Burgess group IIIa.

Britain, no provenance.
L. 17.0 cm., max. W. 6.5 cm.
Purchased Sandy 1948.
1966A34.

51
Fragment of low-flanged looped palstave with
central rib; butt only. Burgess group IIIa.
Britain, no provenance.
extant L. 10.3 cm.
Acquisition details unknown.
1954A22.

52
High-flanged looped palstave with short V-shaped
rib on top of blade on each face. Butt projects
beyond end of flanges. Deep swallow hole in stop
ridge on one side. Burgess group IIIb.
Oxfordshire, Chipping Norton? [Or possibly
Warwickshire, Alcester.]
L. 13.0 cm., max. W. 5.3 cm.
Purchased B. Masters 1965.
Rowlands 1976, no. 827.
1966A41.

53
Looped narrow bladed late type palstave with
projecting stop ridge; butt broken and blade
damaged. Burgess group V.
Surrey, Worthing; found in a field called the
Noacks? about 200 yards from the sea on the east
side of Worthing in 1877.
L. 13.6 cm., max. W. 3.4 cm.
Purchased Birmingham University Medical School
1977.
1973A1355.

54
Looped narrow bladed late type palstave with pro-
jecting stop ridge. Undecorated. Burgess group V.
Bedfordshire, exact provenance unknown; collected
by the vendor's grandfather who lived there.
L. 12.4 cm., blade W. 3.0 cm.
Purchased W.K.J. Osborne 1967.
1967A1307.
Possibly part of a hoard with nos. 55, 56, 61, 62?

55
Looped narrow bladed late type palstave with pro-
jecting stop ridge. Undecorated. Burgess group V.
Bedfordshire, exact provenance unknown; collected
by the vendor's grandfather who lived there.
L. 12.7 cm., blade W. 3.2 cm.
Purchased W.K.J. Osborne 1967.
1967A1308.
Possibly part of a hoard with nos. 54, 56, 61, 62?

56
Narrow bladed late type palstave with projecting
stop ridge; decorated with trident motif. Burgess
group V.
Bedfordshire; collected by vendor's grandfather who
lived there.
L. 14.7 cm., blade W. 3.6 cm.
Purchased W.K.J. Osborne 1967.
1967A1309.
Possibly part of a hoard with nos. 54, 55, 61, 62?

57
Centre winged axe with narrow blade; butt broken
off.
Britain, no provenance.

extant L. 10.4 cm., blade W. 4.3 cm.
Acquisition details unknown.
1954A19.

58
Plain socketed axe with horizontal moulding above
loop but mouth broken beyond that.
Staffordshire, Penkridge near Water Eaton; metal
detected in a field. SJ 906114.
L. 10.5 cm., blade W. 6.0 cm.
Purchased P.A. Corfield 1983.
Watson 1984, 4 no.4.
1983A112.

59
Plain socketed axe with single mouth moulding and
low set loop.
Suffolk, Ipswich.
L. 10.5 cm., blade W. 4.6 cm.
Purchased Birmingham Archaeological Society 1957
ex Barnett bequest..
1957A176.

60
Plain socketed axe with double mouth moulding.
Long hafting ribs in socket, one on each broad
face.
Norfolk, Norwich, Mousehold.
L. 9.9 cm., blade W. 5.0 cm.
Presented by J.R. Ratcliffe 1933, ex T.G. Bayfield of
Norwich.
1933A76.2.

61
Plain socketed axe with double mouth moulding.
Bedfordshire, exact provenance unknown; found by
vendor's grandfather who lived there.
L. 9.1 cm., max. W. 4.4 cm.
Purchased W.K.J. Osborne 1967.
1967A1310.
Possibly part of a hoard with nos. 54, 55, 56, 62?

62
Plain socketed axe with mouth moulding and slight
second moulding below merging with top of loop.
Blade and mouth damaged.
Bedfordshire, exact provenance unknown; found by
vendor's grandfather who lived there.
L. 10.2 cm., max. W. 3.9 cm.
Purchased W.K.J. Osborne 1967.
1967A1311.
Possibly part of a hoard with nos. 54, 55, 56, 61?

63
Three-ribbed socketed axe with side loop and single
mouth moulding. Haft ribs inside socket one in
centre of each broad face.
Warwickshire, Birmingham; found whilst gardening
in Tixall Road, Hall Green. SP 10238005.
L. 10.4 cm., blade W. 5.0 cm.
Purchased R.L. Titmus 1982.
Watson 1984, 4-5, no. 6.
1983A111.

64
Three-ribbed socketed axe with double mouth
moulding. Contained a cut and shaped piece of
wood, presumably from the tip of the haft,
identified as family Rosaceae sub-family Pomoideae
but more precise identification was not possible.
Staffordshire, Wolverhampton; found whilst digging
a garden pond in Keats Road, Bushbury in 1980.

SJ 933025.
L. 10.6 cm., max. W. 4.3 cm.
Purchased in 1980.
Malam 1981, 133–134.
1985A33.

65
Three-ribbed socketed axe. Mouth unevenly cast
and split; large blow hole in the side, behind loop.
England, possibly Yorkshire.
L. 10.6 cm., max. W. 5.3 cm.
Purchased R.T. Clough 1958.
1958A4.

66
Three-ribbed, looped socketed axe with double
mouth moulding. Small blow hole in the side,
behind loop.
Britain, no provenance.
L. 10.8 cm., blade W. 5.0 cm.
Presented Miss W.R. Richardson 1948.
1948A4.8

67
Five-ribbed socketed axe with double mouth
moulding.
Britain, no provenance.
L. 9.8 cm., max. W. 6.0 cm.
Presented Wellcome Trustees 1982.
Stevens 25–26/9/1928 lot 489.
1982A3079.

68
Socketed axe with thick mouth moulding and
smaller horizontal moulding below from which
depends triple rib and pellet decoration.
Gloucestershire, Over.
L. 12.2 cm., max. W. 5.8 cm.
Purchased Birmingham Archaeological Society 1957
ex Barnett bequest.
1957A177.

69
Small Armorican socketed axe. Type Couville.
Britain, no provenance.
L. 7.4 cm., max. W. 2.4 cm.
Presented Dr. G. Rome Hall 1931 ex Greenwell
collection.
1931A68.33.

70
Blade only from a socketed axe.
Britain, no provenance.
extant L. 4.7 cm., max. W. 5.5 cm.
Acquisition details unknown.
1962A399.

71
Pegged, socketed chisel with a collar where the
socket meets the blade recalling the stop ridge on
tanged chisels. Expanded blade.
Britain, no provenance.
L. 5.3 cm., max. W. 3.0 cm.
Acquisition details unknown.
1962A392.

72
Socketed gouge with concavo–convex blade. Two
raised moulded bands about 1 cm. below top of
socket.
Surrey, Purley, Russell Hill. TQ 309621. Found by
Mr. C. Anderson 1898.

L. 9.2 cm.
Presented Mrs. Clayton 1953 ex H.C. Collyer
collection.
Collyer 1908, 208—209 no. 11; Phillips 1967, 17;
Phillips 1968, 133 no. 5.
1953A851.

73
Socketed gouge with concavo-convex blade. Plain
tapering socket.
Britain, no provenance.
L. 7.2 cm.
Acquisition details unknown.
1962A389.

74
Double ended awl made from square section rod
but corners grooved.
Britain, no provenance.
L. 6.0 cm.
Acquisition details unknown.
1962A391.

75
Tanged bifid razor with notch in end of blade and
perforation below. Slight midrib with three raised
lines. Flat tapering tang. Class II.
Middlesex, Brentford, Old England.
L. 7.4 cm., max. W. 4.1 cm.
Acquisition details unknown.
Piggott 1946, 138 no. 46.
1954A21.

76
Razor with hooked tang. Leaf shaped blade with
pronounced midrib giving a lozenge section. Class
IV.
Worcestershire, near Bewdley; metal detected in
1986. SO 774754.
L. 12.5 cm., max. W. 2.8 cm.
Purchased E.B. Smith 1987.
Watson 1988b, 23—25.
1987A218.

77
Cylindrical "bit-spacer" made up of three rings of
six rounded points each; overhanging rim at top
and bottom.
Suffolk, no exact provenance.
max. di. 4.5 cm., H. 2.5 cm.
Purchased from Birmingham Archaeological Society
1957, ex Barnett bequest, ex Acton collection.
1957A187.

78
Trapezoidal hilted rapier; two rivet holes, one with
rivet still in position. Triple arris blade and
grooved omega hilt mark. Burgess and Gerloff
Group III type Methwold.
Nottinghamshire, Chilwell; found "in gravels" at
Attenborough before 1955.
L. 44.1 cm.
Purchased Mrs. O.M. Martin 1966.
Rowlands 1976, no. 1873; Burgess and Gerloff 1981,
no. 329.
1966A30.

79
Flange hilted sword. Leaf shaped blade with central
rib giving concave lozenge section; tip broken off.
Blade faces decorated with six incised lines which
follow blade contour and meet near tip. No ricasso.

Shoulders rounded with three rivet holes in each;
five peg rivets remain. Hilt plate with low flanges
and six rivet holes. Closest type is wide-U swords.
Warwickshire, Solihull; found whilst ploughing in
Powell's Ground, Shirley 1912—1914. SP 12657995.
L. 72.0 cm., blade W. 3.8 cm.
Presented A. Bates 1982.
Watson 1988a, 103—107.
1983A109.

80
Sword; tang and end of blade missing. Gently
curved ricasso; V-shaped butt with three rivet holes
either side. Slight rib along blade edges. Type
Ewart Park.
Britain, no provenance.
extant L. 16.9 cm.
Purchased Sandy 1948.
Colquhoun and Burgess 1988, no. 648.
1948A183.

81
Ogival round-hilted dirk; four rivet holes with four
peg rivets still in place. Decorated with four
incised lines down each side of blade; edges hollow
ground. Trump group I.
Britain, no provenance.
L. 24.0 cm.
Purchased Birmingham University Medical School
1973.
1973A1341.

82
Trapezoidal hilted dirk; tip broken off and one
corner of hilt plate damaged. Two rivet holes, one
with rivet still in position. Trump group II.
Middlesex, Thames, exact location unknown.
extant L. 22.2 cm.
Purchased Birmingham University Medical School
1977 (DCCCXLIX).
Trump 1962, 96 no. 105; Rowlands 1976, no. 1827.
1973A1352.

83
Dirk. Blade with flattened midrib. Hilt plate
broken. Trump group III, Lisburn class.
Kent, Isle of Thanet.
L. 31.7 cm.
Purchased Birmingham University Medical School
1977 (DCCCL).
Trump 1962, 96 no. 82; Rowlands 1976, no. 1714.
1973A1351.

84
Dagger. Blade with midrib; lozenge section. Hilt
plate broken; domed rectangle with two notches.
Late group III or later type.
Britain, no provenance.
L. 13.0 cm.
Acquisition details unknown.
1954A20.

85
Dagger. Tip broken off and tang damaged; remains
of two rivet holes/notches. Triple arris blade.
Britain, no provenance.
extant L. 17.7 cm.
Acquisition details unknown.
1962A390.

86
Socketed side-looped spearhead. Ends of blade and

socket missing; loops damaged.
Staffordshire, Enville; found whilst ploughing in
Haymeadow, Grove Farm 1966. SO 80558835.
extant L. 7.0 cm.
Presented T. Preece 1967.
Gunstone 1972, 50 no. 6; Rowlands 1976, no. 1363;
Vine 1982, no. 813.
1967A1467.

87
Socketed side-looped spearhead. Most of blade
missing. Side loops on socket close to top of blade.
Warwickshire, Kingsbury, Brownings! Croft
[Broomey Croft?]. c. SP 205970.
extant L. 12.3 cm.
Presented John Staunton 1875, ex William Staunton.
Chatwin 1922, 172 no. 8; Rowlands 1976, no. 1401;
Bishop 1977, 127 no. 2; Vine 1982, no. 819.
1885A1494 (1948A4.7).

88
Socketed pegged spearhead with leaf-shaped blade.
Rib damaged on one face. End of socket still
contains wooden haft and rivets.
Britain, no provenance.
L. 28.3 cm., max. W. 5.2 cm.
Purchased Blackmore 1968 ex W.H. Slater English.
1968A1317.

89
Socketed pegged spearhead with very narrow blade.
Britain, no exact provenance.
L. 14.3 cm., max. W. 2.6 cm.
Acquisition details unknown.
1962A393.

90
Tanged arrowhead; barbed. Midrib on blade.
Tapering tang of rectangular section.
Britain, no provenance.
L. 5.0 cm., max. W. 2.4 cm.
Purchased Sandy 1948.
1966A39.

91
Tanged arrowhead. Short rounded barbs. Tapering
tang of crude lozenge section as blade midrib
extends onto tang.
Britain, no provenance.
L. 6.3 cm., max. W. 2.3 cm.
Purchased Sandy 1948.
1966A40.

92
Socketed, pegged arrowhead.
Britain, no provenance.
L. 4.1 cm., max. W. 1.6 cm.
Purchased Sandy 1948.
1966A38.

93
Boat-shaped bow brooch with crude geometric
decoration. Spring and pin missing. Hull and
Hawkes type B (LBA III).
Yorkshire, York.
L. 7.5 cm.
Presented Mrs. E. Prentice 1953.
Hull and Hawkes 1987, 19 no. 8971.
1953A688.

94
Fragment of bracelet of rectangular section with

vertical grooves on outer face only.
Lincolnshire, Tallington, 1965 excavations at
Thurlby's Farm D1 E. section.
extant L. 4.3 cm.
Presented Mr. S. Thurlby 1966.
1991A381.

95
Pair of basket earrings made from sheet bronze;
damaged.
Lincolnshire, Tallington; from excavations at
Thurlby's Farm, Site 17, fill of grave 4.
L. 2.5 cm. and 1.7 cm.
Presented Mr. S. Thurlby 1966.
Clarke 1970, 220a; Davey 1973, 98, 119 nos. 424,
425; Simpson 1976, 233 no. 17.
1966A667.2

96
Casting jet with two runners.
Britain, no provenance.
L. 3.2 cm., di. 2.6 to 3.5 cm.
Acquisition details unknown.
1963A901.

97
Gold twisted ribbon torc with hooked terminals.
Britain or Ireland, no exact provenance.
di. 10.5 cm.
Purchased H.M. Calmann.
Sotheby's 24/2/64 lot 49; Taylor 1980, NLBI 41 =
NLI 283a.
1964A113

98
Gold torc from flange-twisted cruciform bar with
hollow cone terminals soldered on. Tara or Yeovil
type.
Dorset, Hilton hoard, Milton Abbey Estate.
di. 21.8 cm.
Purchased Sothebys 1964 ex Countess of
Portarlington.
Sothebys 6/7/64 lot 99; Taylor 1980, Do 13; Coles
1963, 132 ff.; Roberts 1882, 158–159.
1964A284.

99
Fragment of gold coiled flange-twisted torc with
plain tapering terminal. One terminal and five coils
preserved.
North Shropshire or south Cheshire.
extant L. 15.0 cm., di. 7.2 cm.
Purchased P. Maynard 1973.
1973A1247.

100
Gold alloy torc composed of twelve plaited wires in
six pairs with loop terminals cast onto the ends.
Loops ornamented with two punched wavy lines.
Staffordshire, Glascote; discovered c. 1943.
max. di. 18.0 cm.
Purchased via British Museum as treasure trove
1970.
Painter 1970.
1970A17.
Analysis: Au 29.8%, Ag 41.9%, Cu 27.2%.

101
Gold solid cast penannular earring tapering to plain
terminals; worked to resemble twisted wire.
Britain or Ireland, no provenance.
di. 2.0 cm.

Barnett bequest.
Taylor 1980, NLBI 40.
1935A547.596.

102
Gold solid cast penannular earring tapering to plain
terminals; worked to resemble twisted wire.
Britain or Ireland, no provenance.
di. 2.5 cm.
Barnett bequest.
Taylor 1980, NLBI 37.
1935A547.597.

103
Gold solid cast penannular earring tapering to plain
terminals; worked to resemble twisted wire.
Britain or Ireland, no provenance.
di. 2.5 cm.
Barnett bequest.
Taylor 1980, NLBI 38.
1935A547.598.

104
Gold solid cast penannular earring tapering to plain
terminals; worked to resemble twisted wire.
Britain or Ireland, no provenance.
di. 2.0 cm.
Barnett bequest.
Taylor 1980, NLBI 39.
1935A547.599.

105
Gold penannular earring of circular section
tapering to pointed terminals.
Britain or Ireland, no provenance.
di. 1.2 cm.
Barnett bequest.
Taylor 1980, NLBI 33 = NLI 237j who suggests a
half unit of ring money.
1935A547.592.

106
Penannular ring money; gold over a copper core.
Britain or Ireland, no provenance.
di. 3.0 cm.
Barnett bequest.
Taylor 1980, NLBI 34 = NLI 237g.
1935A547.593.

107
Penannular gold ring money.
Britain or Ireland, no provenance.
di. 1.9 cm.
Barnett bequest.
Taylor 1980, NLBI 35 = NLI 237h.
1935A547.594.

108
Penannular gold, striped ring money.
Britain or Ireland, no provenance.
di. 1.7 cm.
Barnett bequest.
Taylor 1980, NLBI 36 = NLI 237i.
1935A547.595

IRELAND [109—140]

109
Flat axe of so-called ingot type.
Co. Kilkenny, Gerpoint.

L. 11.5 cm., max. W. 6.0 cm., Th. 1.9 cm.
Purchased from Birmingham Archaeological Society
1957, ex Barnett bequest, ex White-King, ex Day?
Harbison 1969 no. 460.
1957A164.

110
Flat axe; undecorated. Type Killaha.
Ireland, no provenance.
L. 11.3 cm., max. W. 8.8 cm., Th. 0.9 cm.
Presented by J.R. Ratcliffe 1930 (marked
DCCCXXX).
1930A104.26.

111
Flat axe. Type Killaha.
Co. Antrim, Ballymena, Fenagh.
L. 13.5 cm., max. W. 8.5 cm.
Purchased from Birmingham Archaeological Society
1957, ex Barnett bequest, ex Knowles.
Sotheby's 17—20/11/1924 lot 589; Harbison 1969 no.
574.
1957A162.1

112
Flat axe; undecorated and probably unfinished.
Type Killaha.
Co. Antrim, no detailed provenance.
L. 15.6 cm., max. W. 9.5 cm., Th. 1.3 cm.
Purchased from Birmingham Archaeological Society
1957, ex Barnett bequest, ex White-King?
Probably Harbison 1969 no. 766.
1957A163.

113
Flat axe; undecorated. Type Killaha.
Co. Cork, Rathcormack.
L. 16.9 cm., max. W. 11.5 cm.
Purchased from Birmingham Archaeological Society
1957, ex Barnett bequest, ex Day.
Harbison 1969 no. 610.
1957A165.

114
Flat axe decorated with vertical zigzags and rows
of punched dots. Ballyvalley type.
Co. Antrim, Glensherry (sic! for Glenwhirry?).
L. 14.9 cm., max. W. 8.2 cm., Th. 1.2 cm.
Purchased from Birmingham Archaeological Society
1957, ex Barnett bequest, ex Knowles.
Sotheby's 17—20/11/1924 lot 593; Harbison 1969 no.
943.
1957A166.

115
Flat axe; undecorated. Ballyvalley type.
Co. Antrim, Glarryford.
L. 10.2 cm., max. W. 4.3 cm., Th. 0.5 cm.
Purchased from Birmingham Archaeological Society
1957, ex Barnett bequest, ex Knowles.
Sotheby's 17—20/11/1924 lot 597b; Harbison 1969 no.
1305.
1957A178.

116
Flat axe; undecorated. Ballyvalley type.
Co. Antrim, Port of Glenon.
L. 8.8 cm., max. W. 4.6 cm., Th. 0.6 cm.
Purchased Birmingham Archaeological Society 1957,
ex Barnett bequest, ex Knowles.
Sotheby's 17—20/11/1924 lot 597; Harbison 1969 no.
1343.
1957A232.

Ireland

117
Flat axe of dubious authenticity.
Co. Antrim, Belfast.
L. 14.2 cm., max. W. 7.3 cm., Th. 1.6 cm.
Purchased Sandy 1948.
1966A42.

118
Flanged axe. Very slight stop ridge below which
blade is decorated with horizontal rows of oblique
slashes. Type Derryniggin.
Co. Londonderry, Londonderry.
L. 10.8 cm., max. W. 4.8 cm., Th. 1.3 cm.
Purchased Birmingham Archaeological Society 1957,
ex Barnett bequest, ex Knowles.
Sotheby's 17–20/11/1924 lot 604b; Harbison 1969 no.
1882 (where the decoration is not mentioned).
1957A173.

119
Flanged axe with slight stop ridge. Undecorated.
Type Derryniggin.
Co. Antrim, Ardnaglass, Grange Park.
L. 10.9 cm., max. W. 5.8 cm., Th. 1.3 cm.
Purchased Birmingham Archaeological Society 1957,
ex Barnett bequest, ex Knowles.
Sotheby's 17–20/11/1924 lot 604a; Harbison 1969 no.
1868.
1957A172.

120
Haft-flanged axe with very slight stop ridge; one
flange broken off.
Co. Down, no exact provenance.
L. 13.2 cm., max. W. 4.6 cm.
Purchased Sandy 1948.
1966A33.

121
Palstave with flanges extending slightly beyond
stop ridge. Burgess group B.
Co. Wicklow, Glendalough.
L. 14.2 cm., max. W. 5.9 cm.
Purchased Birmingham Archaeological Society 1957,
ex Barnett bequest.
1957A174.

122
Palstave with flanges extending slightly beyond
stop ridge. Burgess group B.
Co. Londonderry, Londonderry.
L. 11.3 cm., max. W. 4.5 cm.
Purchased Birmingham University Medical School
1973 (DCCCXXXVI).
1973A303.

123
Palstave with high flanges extending beyond stop
ridge; shield pattern decoration. Burgess group B/A.
Co. Londonderry, Londonderry.
L. 12.7 cm., max. W. 4.1 cm.
Purchased Birmingham University Medical School
1973 (DCCCXXXV).
1973A302.

124
Small crudely cast palstave with traces of trident
pattern decoration on one face. Burgess group A.
Ireland, no exact provenance.
L. 7.9 cm., max. W. 2.7 cm.

Presented by Dr. G. Rome Hall 1931 ex Wm.
Greenwell collection.
1931A68.34.

125
Unlooped palstave with trident pattern; butt broken.
Burgess group A.
Co. Antrim, Ballymoney.
L. 12.3 cm., max. W. 5.4 cm.
Purchased Birmingham University Medical School
1973 (DCCCXXXVIII), ex Robinson collection no.
1571.
1973A305.

126
Looped palstave with central rib; butt broken.
Burgess group D.
Co. Londonderry, no exact provenance.
L. 12.3 cm., max. W. 6.5 cm.
Purchased Birmingham University Medical School
1973 (DCCCXLI).
1973A304.

127
Looped palstave with curved overhanging stop
ridge; small loop with very even (drilled?)
perforation. Most surfaces filed with a modern tool.
Probably a modern forgery.
Co. Cork, no exact provenance.
L. 12.2 cm., max. W. 4.5 cm.
Purchased Birmingham Archaeological Society 1957,
ex Barnett bequest.
1957A175.1.

128
Bag shaped socketed axe with side loop.
Northern Ireland, no exact provenance.
L. 6.2 cm., max. W. 5.1 cm.
Purchased Sandy 1948.
1966A37.

129
Socketed axe with side loop.
Co. Meath, no exact provenance.
L. 5.0 cm., max. W. 3.5 cm.
Presented by Dr. G. Rome Hall 1931.
1931A68.31

130
Flanged chisel with low flanges and contiguous
flange-stop line.
Ireland, no exact provenance.
L. 9.3 cm., max. W. 2.1 cm.
Purchased Birmingham University Medical School
1973 (DCCCXLIV) ex G.F. Lawrence.
1973A306.

131
Rapier with trapezoidal butt with two rivet holes,
one of which is torn. Midrib on blade. Burgess and
Gerloff Group II type Littleport.
Co. Antrim, Skerry East; found near Reilly's Farm
in 1898.
L. 29.2 cm., max. W. 5.4 cm.
Purchased Birmingham Archaeological Society 1957,
ex Barnett bequest, ex Knowles.
Sotheby's 17–20/11/1924 lot 651; Burgess and Gerloff
1981 no. 173.
1957A149.

132
Flange-hilted sword, the hilt attached separately;
three rivet holes in hilt plate and two in shoulder.
Ricasso. Blade has a central thickening and a
shallow groove along edge. Eogan class 4.
Co. Roscommon, near Boyle.
L. 46.3 cm., max. W. 3.5 cm.
Purchased Birmingham Archaeological Society 1957,
ex Barnett bequest.
Possibly Eogan 1965 no. 245.
1957A148.

133
Dagger of lentoid section; tip broken off.
Northern Ireland, no exact provenance.
L. 18.8 cm., max. W. 3.1 cm.
Presented by Wellcome Trustees 1982 (lot 218/2 but
sale and date unknown).
1989A18.

134
Pegged socketed spear head with leaf shaped blade.
Taylorstown (Co. unknown).
L. 22.1 cm., max. W. 2.8 cm.
Purchased Birmingham Archaeological Society 1957,
ex Barnett bequest, ex Knowles.
Sotheby's 17–20/11/1924 lot 646.
1957A179.

135
Pegged socketed spear head with leaf shaped blade.
Co. Antrim, Glenwhirry.
L. 13.8 cm., max. W. 3.5 cm.
Purchased Birmingham Archaeological Society 1957,
ex Barnett bequest, ex Knowles.
Sotheby's 17–20/11/1924 lot 646c.
1957A181.

136
Small pegged socketed spear head with two large,
almost square, peg holes. Small ovoid blade and
wide socket.
Ireland, no exact provenance.
L. 9.3 cm., max. W. 2.3 cm.
Purchased Birmingham Archaeological Society 1957,
ex Barnett bequest, ex Knowles.
Sotheby's 17–20/11/1924 lot 646b.
1957A180.1

137
Pegged socketed arrow head with triangular blade
and midrib on both faces.
Ireland, provenance illegible.
L. 4.5 cm., max. W. 1.5 cm.
Acquisition details not recorded.
1913A85.

138
Three small annular rings of flattened section.
Ireland, no exact provenance.
External Di. 2.6, 3.2 and 3.5 cm. respectively.
Presented by Dr. G. Rome Hall 1931, ex Wm.
Greenwell collection.
1931A68.35; 1931A68.36; 1931A68.37

139
Gold cup-ended dress fastener terminal with incised
line decoration.
Co. Tipperary, Bog of Cullen.
Di. 9.9 – 10.2 cm.
Purchased Sotheby's 1964, ex Countess of
Portarlington.

Sotheby's 6/7/64 lot 98; Taylor 1980, CoTp 11; Coles
1963, 133–134, pl. xv; Roberts 1882, 159; Vallancey
1804, pl. xvi fig. 6; *Archaeologia* 3 (1775), 357, pl.
19.
1964A283

140
Gold ring made from circular section rod tapering
towards terminals which are twisted over each
other.
Ireland, no exact provenance.
Di. 3.5 cm.
Bequeathed by T.G. Barnett 1935.
Taylor 1980, NLI 323.
1935A547.600

AUSTRIA [141–142]

141
Serpentine fibula; pin lost.
Austria, Hallstatt.
L. 9.8 cm.
Purchased Sandy 1948.
1948A134.

142
Annular bracelet of oval section with deep knobbed
and ribbed decoration.
Austria, no exact provenance.
max. Di. 8.5 cm.
Purchased Sandy 1948.
1948A131.

BELGIUM [143]

143
Socketed axe with double mouth moulding and
wing decoration. Loop miscast and not fully joined
up; two blow holes, one near the loop and a larger
one on the other side near the seam.
Namur, Chateau Yvoir.
L. 13.4 cm., max. W. 3.9 cm.
Purchased Blackmore 1968, ex John Jones March
1869.
1968A1268.

FRANCE [144–220]

144
Flat axe.
Vaucluse, Carpentras.
L. 8.0 cm., max. W. 2.9 cm.
Purchased Blackmore 1968 (24, C.4).
1968A1241.

145
Flanged axe.
Alpes-Maritimes, Antibes.
L. 20.3 cm., max. W. 6.7 cm.
Purchased Blackmore 1968 (23, C.3).
1968A1242.

146
Flanged axe.
Paris.
L. 16.2 cm., max. W. 8.0 cm.
Purchased Blackmore 1968 (21, C.1).
1968A1243.

France

147
Flanged axe.
Lot et Garonne, Agen. Said to have been found with 148 below.
L. 14.4 cm., max. W. 5.6 cm.
Purchased Blackmore 1968 (29, C.8).
1968A1245.

148
Flanged axe.
Lot et Garonne, Agen. Said to have been found with 147 above.
L. 20.0 cm., max. W. 5.3 cm.
Purchased Blackmore 1968 (27, C.6).
1968A1246.

149
Flanged axe.
Lot et Garonne, Agen.
L. 14.7 cm., max. W. 4.6 cm.
Purchased Blackmore 1968 (28, C.7).
1968A1247.

150
Flanged axe.
France, no exact provenance; however this type comes almost exclusively from the south-east (see Chardenoux and Courtois 1979, 46).
L. 15.1 cm., max. W. 8.8 cm.
Purchased Blackmore 1968 (32, C.13).
1968A1244.

151
Flanged axe with circular notch in butt for haft dowel; (for the type see Chardenoux and Courtois 1979, 53ff.).
Gard, Nimes.
L. 15.8 cm., max. W. 5.3 cm.
Purchased Blackmore 1968 (22, C.2).
1968A1248.

152
Flanged axe.
France, no exact provenance.
L. 9.7 cm., max. W. 4.4 cm.
Purchased Blackmore 1968 (30, C.9).
1968A1251.

153
Undecorated palstave with low flanges and notch in butt for haft dowel. Haguenau/Middle Rhenish type (see Sandars 1957, 70).
France, no exact provenance.
L. 21.2 cm., blade W. 5.7 cm.
Purchased Blackmore 1968 (3, W.B.16).
1968A1255.

154
Undecorated palstave with low flanges and prominent stop ridge. Haguenau/Middle Rhenish type (Sandars 1957, 70).
France, no exact provenance.
L. 13.1 cm., blade W. 3.5 cm.
Purchased Blackmore 1968 (33, C.10).
1968A1252.

155
Palstave made from halves of two different moulds and incorrectly aligned; stop ridge curved on one side, straight on other. Central rib on both faces.
Indre et Loire, Tours.
L. 16.6 cm., blade W. 4.7 cm.

Purchased Pitt-Rivers 1983, ex Roots collection.
Christies 20/4/1891.
1983A812.

156
Palstave with shield pattern and midrib below.
France, no exact provenance.
L. 17.4 cm., blade W. 6.9 cm.
Purchased Blackmore 1968 (34, C.12).
1968A1253.

157
Low flanged palstave with trident decoration. Trident decoration is normally regarded as typical of Normandy and examples from Brittany are rare (see Briard 1965, 115).
Finistere, Quimper.
L. 14.3 cm., blade W. 6.2 cm.
Purchased Blackmore 1968 (36, W.B. 10).
1968A1254.

158
Looped palstave with prominent central rib on blade; loop broken.
Manche, Valognes.
L. 18.8 cm., blade W. 4.6 cm.
Purchased Blackmore 1968 (34, W.B. 11).
1968A1256.

159
Centre winged axe with crescentic notch in butt for haft dowel; low stop ridge. This type is common in central Italy (see Bietti Sestieri 1973, 396ff.) but does occur infrequently in south and central France (Chardenoux and Courtois 1979, 94).
Aude, Narbonne.
L. 17.5 cm., blade W. 5.5 cm.
Purchased Blackmore 1968 (6, C.16).
1968A1257.

160
Centre winged axe with deep notch in butt for haft dowel. Type Grigny. For distribution of this type see Chardenoux and Courtois 1979, 93.
Meurthe-et-Moselle, Toul.
L. 19.0 cm., blade W. 5.1 cm.
Purchased Blackmore 1968 (5, C.15).
1968A1258.

161
End winged axe with high stop ridge. This is an Italian early Iron Age type; for another similar example from France see Chardenoux and Courtois 1979, pl. 41, no. 712A.
Alpes-Maritimes, Antibes.
L. 18.5 cm., blade W. 6.9 cm.
Purchased Blackmore 1968 (10, C.19).
1968A1259.

162
End winged axe with no stop ridge. Italian early Iron Age type.
Vaucluse, Carpentras.
L. 17.8 cm., blade W. 7.2 cm.
Purchased Blackmore 1968 (7, C.17).
1968A1260.

163
End winged axe. Probably a modern forgery.
France, no exact provenance.
L. 14.8 cm., blade W. 5.2 cm.
Purchased Birmingham University Medical School

1973 (DCCCXLII).
1973A309.

164
Looped centre winged axe with high in-turned
wings; flattened notch in butt for haft dowel.
Dordogne, Perigueux.
L. 13.7 cm., blade W. 3.8 cm.
Purchased Pitt-Rivers 1983, ex Roots collection.
Christies 20/4/1891 lot 64.
1983A815.

165
Looped centre winged axe; no notch in butt.
France, no exact provenance.
L. 15.1 cm., blade W. 4.5 cm.
Purchased Blackmore 1968 (8, W.B. 14).
1968A1261.

166
Socketed axe with bevelled rim and thickened
mouth moulding; two narrow raised bands below.
Prominent casting seams and remains of casting
jets in socket. Type Dahouet.
Morbihan, an island near Belz.
L. 12.8 cm., blade W. 4.2 cm.
Purchased Blackmore 1968 (26, 28 ETS 12), ex E.T.
Stevens.
1968A1269.

167
Socketed axe with unfinished rim, thickened mouth
moulding and single raised band below on faces
only. Wide loop. Prominent casting seams and
remains of casting jet in socket. Casting flaw in
one corner of blade. Type Trehou.
France, no exact provenance.
L. 13.2 cm., blade W. 3.3 cm.
Purchased Blackmore 1975.
1975A112.

168
Socketed axe with ragged rim and thickened mouth
moulding. Raised band on faces only with three
raised pellets below. Very thin walled and there are
five blow holes at various points. Type Trehou.
Morbihan, an island near Belz.
L. 12.7 cm., max. W. 3.2 cm.
Purchased Blackmore 1968 (22).
1968A1270.

169
Socketed axe with thickened mouth moulding and
single raised band below on faces only. Type
Trehou.
France, "Brittany".
L. 12.6 cm., max. W. 3.2 cm.
Purchased Birmingham University Medical School
1973 (DCCCXXXIII).
1973A1354.

170
Socketed axe with mouth moulding and raised band
below on faces only. Prominent casting ridge
remains on sides and on cutting edge; traces of
casting jets in socket. Two blow holes in one side.
Type Trehou.
France, no exact provenance.
L. 13.3 cm., max. W. 3.7 cm.
Found unaccessioned in store; possibly ex Sandy.
1987A346.

171
Socketed axe with mouth moulding and raised band
below on faces only. Casting ridge remains on sides
and on cutting edge. Type Trehou.
France, "Brittany".
L. 12.8 cm., max. W. 3.2 cm.
Found unaccessioned in store; possibly ex
Birmingham University Medical School.
1987A347.

172
Socketed axe with mouth moulding and raised band
below on faces only. Casting ridges on sides and on
cutting edge; remains of casting jets in socket.
Type Trehou.
Gironde, Bordeaux.
L. 12.9 cm., max. W. 3.4 cm.
Purchased Pitt-Rivers 1983, ex Lawrence 1898.
1983A531.

173
Socketed axe with mouth moulding and indistinct
raised band below. Remains of casting jets in
socket. Type Trehou.
France, no exact provenance.
L. 12.8 cm., max. W. 3.5 cm.
Purchased Pitt-Rivers 1983.
1983A532.

174
Socketed axe with mouth moulding and raised band
below on faces only. Part of upper portion,
including loop, lost. Prominent casting seams on
edges and on cutting edge. Type Trehou.
France, no exact provenance.
L. 13.3 cm., max. W. 3.5 cm.
Purchased Blackmore 1975.
1975A114.

175
Socketed axe with mouth moulding; undecorated.
Thin loop. Casting ridges on sides. Type Plurien.
France, no exact provenance.
L. 12.1 cm., max. W. 3.1 cm.
Purchased Blackmore 1975.
1975A113.

176
Socketed axe with mouth moulding; undecorated.
Prominent casting seams down sides and on cutting
edge. Type Plurien.
France, "Brittany".
L. 11.6 cm., max. W. 3.3 cm.
Purchased Birmingham University Medical School
1973 (DCCCXXXVII).
1973A308.

177
Miniature socketed axe with mouth moulding and
raised band below. Two vertical raised ribs on each
face and raised ring and dot motifs - one in centre
of face at level of loop and one in each corner of
blade. Part of rim and one side broken away.
Casting debris lodged inside loop and remains of
casting jet on one side of socket. Type Couville.
France, no exact provenance.
L. 7.1 cm., max. W. 2.2 cm.
Purchased Blackmore 1968 (21, C.27).
1968A1274.

178
Miniature socketed axe with mouth moulding and

France

indistinct raised band below on faces only. Two vertical ribs on faces of blade, not quite parallel. Remains of casting ridge on cutting edge. Type Couville.
France, no exact provenance.
L. 7.3 cm., max. W. 2.3 cm.
Purchased Blackmore 1968 (18, C.25).
1968A1272.

179
Miniature socketed axe with mouth moulding and indistinct raised band below on faces only. Type Couville.
Pas de Calais, Boulogne-sur-Mer; found 18th May 1867.
L. 7.5 cm., max. W. 2.5 cm.
Purchased Blackmore 1968 (17, W.B. 18).
1968A1273.

180
Miniature socketed axe with mouth moulding and indistinct raised band below. Most of the casting seam removed. Type Couville.
France, "Brittany".
L. 7.4 cm., max. W. 2.4 cm.
Purchased Birmingham University Medical School 1973 (DCCCXXXIV).
1973A307.

181
Miniature socketed axe with mouth moulding; undecorated. Prominent casting seam, large blow hole and crack on unlooped side. Type Couville.
France, "Brittany".
L. 7.4 cm., max. W. 2.5 cm.
No acquisition details.
1962A394.

182
Miniature socketed axe with mouth moulding and raised band below. Casting seams remain on sides. Type Couville.
Somme, Abbeville; collected in 1866.
L. 7.9 cm., max. W. 2.7 cm.
Purchased Blackmore 1968.
1968A1271.

183
Miniature socketed axe with mouth moulding; mouth damaged. Poorly cast. Type Couville.
France, "Brittany".
L. 7.8 cm., max. W. 2.6 cm.
Found unaccessioned in store; at one time in the Bateman collection.
1987A349.

184
Miniature socketed axe with mouth moulding; undecorated. Prominent casting ridges and casting debris adhering to surfaces; blow hole below moulding. Type Couville.
France, "Brittany".
L. 8.0 cm., max. W. 2.9 cm.
Purchased Pitt-Rivers 1983.
1983A533.

185
Miniature socketed axe with poorly fashioned uneven mouth moulding; undecorated. Prominent casting seams. Type Maure.
France, "Brittany".

L. 5.0 cm., max. W. 1.6 cm.
Purchased Birmingham Archaeological Society 1957, ex Barnett bequest.
1957A184.

186
Miniature socketed axe with uneven mouth moulding; undecorated. One corner of mouth missing. Remains of casting seam on cutting edge. Type Maure.
France, "Brittany".
L. 4.6 cm., max. W. 1.4 cm.
Purchased Birmingham Archaeological Society 1957, ex Barnett bequest.
1957A185.

187
Socketed axe with bevelled mouth moulding, two raised bands and wing decoration. Small loop; blade uneven.
Somme, Abbeville.
L. 11.0 cm., max. W. 3.6 cm.
Presented Dr. G. Rome Hall 1931.
1931A68.30.

188
Shaft hole axe with raised edges imitating wings. Decoration consists of two long and one short raised ribs. Casting scar projects from heel.
Dordogne, Perigueux.
L. 15.4 cm., max. W. 5.6 cm., shaft hole 2.7 x 3.7 cm.
Purchased Pitt-Rivers 1983, ex Roots collection. Christies 20/4/1891.
1983A818.

189
Cast shaft hole axe of simple form. Shaft hole slightly tapered.
France, no exact provenance.
L. 16.8 cm., max. W. 7.0 cm., shaft hole 2.9 x 3.2 cm.
Purchased Blackmore 1968.
1968A1249.

190
Cast shaft hole axe of simple form.
Var, Draguignan.
L. 20.5 cm., max. W. 7.0 cm., shaft hole 2.7 x 3.9 cm.
Purchased Blackmore 1968.
1968A1250.

191
Tanged knife with convex curving blade; thickened concave back. Made in a two piece mould and the two halves not correctly aligned.
Savoie, Lac du Bourguet.
L. 14.9 cm.
Purchased Pitt-Rivers 1983, ex Lawrence June 1898.
1983A329.

192
Tanged leaf shaped sword with central rib and ground edges. Hilt hammered into solid tang of square section bulging to a knob at the end. Two rivet holes in shoulders, one each side.
France, no exact provenance.
L. 47.5 cm., max. blade W. 3.8 cm.
Purchased Blackmore 1968.
1968A1263.

17

France

193
Hollow hilted sword, the blade and bronze hilt made separately. The hollow hilt was cast in one piece and then attached to the blade by three rivets through one side of the hilt grip and a further three rivets through both sides of the shoulders. The grip has three raised ridges. The pommel is circular and flat and has a hole in the crude central boss. Leaf shaped blade. No ricasso. Several casting flaws on hilt and blade.
France, no exact provenance.
L. 70 cm., max. W. at shoulder 5.4 cm.
Purchased Blackmore 1968.
1968A1264.

194
Flange hilted sword with four rivet holes in shoulders, two each side, and one rivet hole at base of hilt grip. End of hilt missing. Narrow blade with central rib to either side of which is a single incised line. Ground edges. No ricasso.
Lot et Garonne, Agen.
L. 67 cm., max. W. 3.9 cm.
Purchased Blackmore 1968.
1968A1262.

195
Dagger with bronze hilt cast separately over a clay core and attached to the blade by eight rivets through the shoulders; there is a further rivet through the centre of the pommel. Blade has a broad central rib. Rhone type (see Sandars 1950, 50ff.).
France, no exact provenance.
L. 23.5 cm., max. W. 5.5 cm.
Purchased Blackmore 1968.
1968A1240.

196
Pegged socketed spear head.
France, no exact provenance.
L. 14.1 cm., max. W. 2.6 cm.
Purchased Blackmore 1968.
1968A1267.

197
Pegged socketed spear head with prominent central rib and lower ribs to each side. Blow hole near base of socket on one side.
France, no exact provenance.
L. 19.4 cm., max. W. 3.5 cm.
Purchased Blackmore 1968.
1968A1266.

198
Open sectioned bracelet with flattened out-turned terminals. Decorated with alternating groups of long and short opposing oblique lines.
Savoie, Lac du Bourget.
max. Di. 7.5 cm.
Purchased Pitt-Rivers 1983, ex Lawrence June 1898.
1983A402.

199
Circular section bracelet with flattened slightly out-turned terminals. Traces of incised line decoration.
Savoie, Lac du Bourget.
max. Di. 5.4 cm.
Purchased Pitt-Rivers 1983, ex Lawrence March 1898.
1983A403.

200
Penannular bracelet with plain terminals; circular section. Decorated with groups of incised lines separated by X's.
Savoie, Lac du Bourget.
max. Di. 7.0 cm.
Purchased Pitt-Rivers 1983, ex Lawrence 1898.
1983A1055.

201
Plain D-section bracelet. One terminal tapers to a rounded point, other broken.
Savoie, Lac du Bourget.
max. Di. 5.0 cm.
Purchased Pitt-Rivers 1983, ex Lawrence March 1898.
1983A425.

202
Penannular bracelet of D-shaped section decorated with nine groups of incised lines. Possibly a pair with 203. [See also 544 below.]
France, no exact provenance.
max. Di. 7.1 cm.
Purchased Blackmore 1968.
1968A1264.1

203
Penannular bracelet of D-shaped section decorated with nine groups of incised lines. Possibly a pair with 202.
France, no exact provenance.
max. Di. 7.1 cm.
Purchased Blackmore 1968.
1968A1265.

204
Penannular bracelet of rectangular section with crude (broken?) slightly tapered terminals. Outer face lightly engraved with panels of lozenges and zig zags between vertical lines with ladder pattern.
France, no exact provenance.
max. Di. 7.6 cm.
Purchased Blackmore 1968.
1968A1302.

205
Penannular bracelet of crescentic section; coiled terminals. Decorated with panels of vertical and diagonal lines with ring and dot motif between. Restored from three fragments. Possibly a pair with 206.
France, no exact provenance.
max. Di. 7.7 cm.
Purchased Blackmore 1968 (b).
1968A1294.

206
Penannular bracelet of crescentic section; coiled terminals. Decorated with panels of vertical and diagonal lines with ring and dot motif between. Restored from two fragments. Possibly a pair with 205.
France, no exact provenance.
max. Di. 8.3 cm.
Purchased Blackmore 1968 (a).
1968A1295.

207
Penannular bracelet of crescentic section; coiled terminals. Decorated with panels of vertical and diagonal lines with ring and dot motif between.

Restored from two fragments.
France, no provenance.
max. Di. 7.7 cm.
Purchased Blackmore 1968.
1968A1300.

208
Penannular bracelet of circular section with
moulded buffer terminals.
France, no exact provenance.
max. Di. 8.9 cm.
Purchased Blackmore 1968.
1968A1292.

209
Annular bracelet of rectangular section with
shallow ribbed decoration.
France, no exact provenance.
max. Di. 6.0 cm.
Purchased Blackmore 1968.
1968A1301.

210
Annular bracelet of solid oval section with deep
knobbed and ribbed decoration.
France, no exact provenance.
max. Di. 7.9 cm.
Purchased Blackmore 1968.
1968A1296.

211
Annular hollow cast armlet with knobbed
decoration. Two of the knobs, on opposite sides, are
perforated vertically. Inside of ring open.
France, no exact provenance.
max. Di. 13.9 cm.
Purchased Blackmore 1968.
1968A1304.

212
Spiral bracelet of oval section with thickened knob
terminals. Decorated with three horizontal engraved
lines; short vertical lines on terminals.
France, no exact provenance.
max. Di. 5.3 cm.
Purchased Blackmore 1968.
1968A1299.

213
Spiral bracelet of roughly circular section with
plain tapering terminals. Undecorated.
France, no exact provenance.
max. Di. 7.8 cm.
Purchased Blackmore 1968.
1968A1293.

214
Spiral bracelet of thick circular section. Plain
terminals decorated with incised lines. Ends of
terminals each incised with an X.
France, no exact provenance.
max. Di. 9.1 cm.
Purchased Blackmore 1968.
1968A1303.

215
Spiral bracelet of variably square and polygonal
section. Plain slightly expanded terminals.
Undecorated.
France, no exact provenance.
max. Di. 9.0 cm.
Purchased Blackmore 1968.

1968A1298.

216
Spiral bracelet of oval section. Plain slightly
tapering terminals. Undecorated.
France, no provenance.
max. Di. 8.5 cm.
Purchased Blackmore 1968.
1968A1297.

217
Pectoral made from bronze strips riveted together
and with two suspension rings. Decorated with
punched dots, crescents and cut-out crosses. Now in
17 pieces.
Savoie, Lac du Bourget.
Purchased Pitt-Rivers 1983.
1983A534.

218
Group of twelve bronze beads.
France, no exact provenance.
Di. c. 1.3 cm.
Purchased Blackmore 1968.
1968A1313.

219
Fragment comprising an open cylindrical shaft
from which extends a hollow rectangular section
cantilever.
Cote d'Or, Mailly.
L. 6.9 cm.
Purchased Pitt-Rivers 1983.
1983A822.

220
Bell in the form of a two-petalled tulip with
suspension loop at closed end; no pea or clapper.
Attached is a fifteen link chain made up of simple
open rings of metal.
France, no exact provenance.
L. 3.6 cm.
Purchased Pitt-Rivers 1983, ex Lawrence June 1898.
1983A824.

GERMANY [221–222]

221
Flanged axe.
Nassau.
L. 12.1 cm., blade W. 5.1 cm.
Purchased Blackmore 1968, ex Sir Alexander Malet.
1968A1494.

222
Armorican socketed axe with bevelled mouth
moulding. Casting ridges on edges and blade
unsharpened. Clay plug in socket.
Nassau.
L. 12.6 cm., blade W. 3.1 cm.
Purchased Blackmore 1968.
1968A1493.

GREECE [223]

223
Disc-topped pin with two sub-spherical swellings
below. Tip missing.
Greece, no exact provenance.

L. 6.7 cm.
Acquisition details unknown; probably acquired prior to 1939.
1963A174.

HUNGARY [224–225]

224
Centre winged axe with small high wings set low down blade.
Baja.
L. 11.4 cm., blade W. 3.1 cm.
Acquisition details unknown; marked C.H. 9.
1989A15.

225
Shaft hole battle axe with raised flanges along edge of blade. Flat circular butt with central spike and six raised pellets around. End of blade broken off. This type is typical of MBA Tumulus culture, Koszider phase; see Sulimirski 1964, 184; Gimbutas 1965, 72.
Hungary, no exact provenance.
L. 19.8 cm., H. shaft hole 6.5 cm., Di. shaft hole 1.6 cm., Di. butt 5.1 - 5.6 cm.
Presented Wellcome Trustees 1982 (A25963).
Sotheby's 6–7/12/1920 lot 125.
1989A14.

ITALY [226–234]

226
Flanged axe with notch in butt for haft dowel.
Rome.
L. 9.8 cm., max. W. 4.0 cm.
Purchased Birmingham University Medical School 1973 (DCCCXXXII).
1973A311.

227
Heavy centre winged axe with irregular notch in butt for haft dowel. Two of wings, which almost meet, are damaged. Very slight stop ridge at base of wings.
Italy, no exact provenance.
L. 20.8 cm., max. W. 5.0 cm.
Purchased Birmingham University Medical School 1973 (DCCCXLV).
1973A312.

228
End winged axe with spade shaped blade.
Italy, no exact provenance.
L. 19.2 cm., max. W. 9.5 cm.
Purchased Birmingham University Medical School 1973 (DCCCXLIII).
1973A1350.

229
End winged axe with expanded blade. Upper part of blade decorated with concentric circles and punched dots; wings decorated with concentric circles, lines and punched dots. Blade very thin and of no functional use.
Central Italy, no exact provenance.
L. 20.4 cm., max. W. 11.1 cm.
Purchased Blackmore 1968 (C.18).
1968A1504.

230
Pegged socketed spear head with leaf shaped blade and octagonal socket.
Italy, no exact provenance.
L. 26.8 cm., max. W. 5.8 cm.
Purchased Blackmore 1968.
1968A1503.

231
Pegged socketed spear head with ogival blade and 12-sided socket. Decorated with oblique slashes on edges of socket above and below peg hole.
Italy, no exact provenance.
L. 21.5 cm., max. W. 3.8 cm.
Purchased Blackmore 1968.
1968A1502.

232
Pegged socketed spear head with ogival blade and circular socket.
Cervetri.
L. 19.4 cm., max. W. 4.9 cm.
Purchased Birmingham University Medical School 1973 (DCCCLII).
1973A1353.

233
Large ring (armilla) of circular section decorated with six thickened beads.
Italy, no exact provenance.
Di. 14.5 cm.
Purchased Blackmore 1968.
1968A1314.

234
Large ring (armilla) of circular section decorated with six thickened biconical beads.
Italy, no provenance.
Di. 14.5 cm.
Purchased Blackmore 1968.
1968A1315.

DENMARK AND SWEDEN [235–243]

235
Faceted socketed axe with hexagonal mouth. Small raised band at level of top of loop. Remains of wooden haft inside.
Denmark, no exact provenance.
L. 10.2 cm., blade W. 6.2 cm.
Purchased Pitt-Rivers 1983, ex Lawrence 1896.
1983A846.

236
Rectangular razor with curled over tang.
Denmark, no exact provenance.
L. 9.5 cm., max. W. 2.0 cm.
Purchased Pitt-Rivers 1983.
1983A847.

237
Squat rectangular razor with tang cast as if curled over into a spiral.
Denmark, no exact provenance.
L. 8.4 cm., W. 3.0 cm.
Purchased Pitt-Rivers 1983, ex Bryce-Wright.
1983A247.

238
Rectangular razor with curled over tang. Incised

decoration along upper part of blade on one side only.
Denmark, no exact provenance.
L. 8.5 cm., W. 1.8 cm.
Purchased Pitt-Rivers 1983.
1983A242.

239
Sword fragment preserving part of mid section of blade only. Central rib on each face with four incised parallel lines to either side. Edges badly nicked.
Denmark, no exact provenance.
L. 17.2 cm., W. 3.4 cm.
No acquisition details; marked 6175.
1989A16.

240
Stud consisting of two circular discs joined by a length of circular section rod. Face of upper disc decorated with three raised concentric circles. Lower disc plain and slightly smaller.
Jutland, supposedly from a grave.
H. 1.1 cm., Di. upper disc 1.2 cm.
Presented Mrs. Giles 1930, ex Wilson King.
1930A389.

241
Flanged axe.
Sweden, no exact provenance.
L. 14.5 cm., max. W. 4.2 cm.
Purchased Blackmore 1968.
1968A1500.

242
Hammer flanged axe. The flanges form a V-shaped stop ridge below which the blade is narrow, waisted and faceted flaring to a highly expanded cutting edge. Butt notched for a haft dowel.
Sweden, no exact provenance.
L. 12.3 cm., max. W. 3.4 cm.
Purchased Blackmore 1968 (C.35).
1968A1495.

243
Socketed axe with raised collar around neck. U-shaped moulding on top of faceted blade. V-shaped haft rib in bottom of socket.
Sweden, no exact provenance.
L. 5.6 cm., max. W. 4.0 cm.
Purchased Blackmore 1968.
1968A1501.

SPAIN [244–246]

244
Single edged in-curving sword with sunken channels along thicker top edge of blade. Hilt curves back on itself with hook-like projection on lower edge and flat barrel shaped terminal. Four peg rivets.
Spain, no exact provenance.
L. 54.0 cm., max. W. blade 5.0 cm., L. hilt 10.8 cm.
Purchased Pitt-Rivers 1983.
1983A811.

245
Iron socketed spear head with narrow lanceolate blade and pronounced midrib on both faces. Tip is rhomboidal in section. Steeply tapering socket.

Blade damaged.
Spain, no exact provenance.
L. 37.8 cm., max. W. blade 2.8 cm., max. Di. socket 2.2 cm.
Purchased Pitt-Rivers 1983, ex Rollin March 1891 (P.672).
1983A810.

246
Iron pegged socketed spear head with long narrow lanceolate blade and flattened midrib on both faces. Tapering socket with thickened collar near end and remains of one peg hole. Blade and end of socket damaged.
Spain, no exact provenance.
L. 45.6 cm., max. W. blade 2.9 cm., max. Di. socket 2.3 cm.
Purchased Pitt-Rivers 1983.
1983A809.

SWITZERLAND [247–513]

247
Flat axe.
Lake Neuchatel, Estavayer.
L. 14.3 cm., blade W. 5.4 cm., butt W. 2.4 cm.
Purchased Pitt-Rivers 1983, ex Lawrence Nov. 1898.
1983A357.

248
Flanged axe with hemispherical blade. One side and one edge covered in concreted deposit.
Swiss Lakes, no provenance.
L. 13.0 cm., blade W. 6.0 cm., butt W. 1.8 cm.
Purchased Pitt-Rivers 1983 ex Roots collection.
Christies 20/4/1891.
1983A358.

249
Centre-winged axe with high flanges bent over to produce socket-like clamp. Notch in butt for hafting. Narrow blade.
Lake Neuchatel.
L. 13.5 cm., max. W. 4.2 cm., butt W. 1.9 cm.
Purchased Pitt-Rivers 1983.
1983A359.

250
Heavy, looped, centre-winged axe with high flanges; no hafting notch in butt.
Lake Neuchatel.
L. 14.5 cm., blade W. 4.8 cm., butt W. 2.2 cm.
Purchased Pitt-Rivers 1983.
1983A360.

251
Square section chisel.
Lake Neuchatel, Cortaillod.
L. 10.7 cm.
Purchased Pitt-Rivers 1983.
1983A250.

252
Square section chisel with straight cutting edge and bevelled tang.
Swiss Lakes, no provenance.
L. 8.0 cm.
Purchased Pitt-Rivers 1983.
1983A251.

253
Circular section chisel with narrow blade and
tapering pointed tang.
Swiss Lakes, no provenance.
L. 6.5 cm.
Purchased Pitt-Rivers 1983.
1983A1050.

254
Tapering circular section chisel with blunt pointed
tang.
Swiss Lakes, no provenance.
L. 5.4 cm.
Purchased Pitt-Rivers 1983.
1983A252.

255
Rectangular section chisel with rounded cutting
edge, flared haft stop and long pointed tang of
circular section.
Lake Neuchatel.
L. 11.4 cm.
Purchased Pitt-Rivers 1983.
1983A338.

256
Socketed chisel with solid blade and thickened
moulding round socket mouth.
Swiss Lakes, no provenance.
L. 10.5 cm.
Purchased Pitt-Rivers 1983 ex Roots collection.
Christies 20/04/1891.
1983A361.

257
Awl of square section.
Lake Neuchatel.
L. 4.8 cm.
Purchased Worcester Museum 1951.
1951A725.

258
Small pointed awl.
Lake Neuchatel.
L. 3.2 cm.
Purchased Worcester Museum 1951.
1951A726.

259
Double ended awl.
Swiss Lakes, no provenance.
L. 5.4 cm.
Purchased Pitt-Rivers 1983.
1983A339.

260
Heavy needle with eye at one end.
Swiss Lakes, no provenance.
L. 7.8 cm.
Purchased Pitt-Rivers 1983.
1983A1051.

261
Needle with eye through flattened area near end.
Swiss Lakes, no provenance.
L. 6.3 cm.
Purchased Pitt-Rivers 1983.
1983A345.

262
Needle; tip broken.
Lake Neuchatel.

extant L. 4.5 cm.
Purchased Pitt-Rivers 1983.
1983A346.

263
Needle; tips missing at both ends.
Swiss Lakes, no provenance.
L. 6.1 cm.
Purchased Pitt- Rivers 1983.
1983A1052.

264
Side looped socketed hammer of square section
with thickened rim round socket mouth. Four haft
ribs inside socket, one on each face.
Lake Neuchatel.
H. 5.5 cm.
Purchased Pitt-Rivers 1983.
1983A423.

265
Fragment of shaft hole hammer broken through
shaft hole.
Swiss Lakes, no provenance.
extant L. 4.2 cm.
Purchased Pitt-Rivers 1983.
1983A424.

266
Fragment of sickle.
Lake Neuchatel.
extant L. 9.5 cm.
Purchased Worcester Museum 1951.
1951A722.

267
U-shaped sickle with circular hafting hole in tang
and projecting stop on outer edge.
Lake Bienne, Locraz.
L. 12.0 cm.
Purchased Pitt-Rivers 1983 ex Lawrence 1898.
1983A362.

268
U-shaped sickle with circular hafting hole in tang;
no stop. Irregular hole through blade from casting
flaw.
Lake Neuchatel.
L. 13.0 cm.
Purchased Pitt-Rivers 1983
1983A363.

269
Sickle with hafting slot in tang and small
projecting stop.
Lake Neuchatel.
L. 11.2 cm.
Purchased Pitt-Rivers 1983.
1983A364.

270
Fragment of saw blade with perforation near one
end.
Lake Neuchatel.
L. 3.9 cm., W. 2.7 cm.
Purchased Pitt-Rivers 1983.
1983A241.

271
Knife with straight cutting edge and straight,
thickened back; rectangular section tang beaten to
ribbon at end and bent over.

Lake Bienne, Locraz.
L. 8.3 cm.
Purchased Pitt-Rivers 1983 ex Lawrence 1898.
1983A335.

272
Knife with concave cutting edge and convex,
thickened back decorated with incised parallel lines
and crosses; rectangular section tang.
Swiss Lakes, no provenance.
L. 13.2 cm.
Purchased Pitt-Rivers 1983 ex Roots collection.
Christies 20/4/1891.
1983A326.

273
Tanged knife with thickened back; oblique burrs on
tang.
Swiss Lakes, no provenance.
L. 14.7 cm.
Purchased Pitt-Rivers 1983.
Sotheby's 03/03/1898 lot 519.
1983A330.

274
Tanged knife with convex blade and thickened
back; oblique burrs on tang. Blade decorated with
incised lines, concentric circles, semi-circles and
punched dots.
Swiss Lakes, no provenance.
L. 19.9 cm.
Purchased Pitt-Rivers 1983.
1983A331.

275
Tanged knife with straight cutting edge turned up
at tip and steeply convex, thickened back decorated
with incised lines and crosses. Tang beaten to a
ribbon at end and bent over.
Lake Neuchatel.
L. 21.4 cm.
Purchased Pitt-Rivers 1983.
1983A332.

276
Tanged knife with elongated S-shaped blade and
thickened back decorated with groups of incised
lines; short tang.
Swiss Lakes, no provenance.
L. 11.2 cm.
Purchased Pitt-Rivers 1983.
1983A333.

277
Tanged knife with small very elongated blade; back
not thickened.
Lake Neuchatel.
L. 8.9 cm.
Purchased Pitt-Rivers 1983.
1983A334.

278
Tanged knife with slightly curving blade and
thickened back; rectangular section tang tapering to
a chisel end. Tang separated from blade by a raised
collar.
Lake Neuchatel.
L. 15.6 cm.
Purchased Pitt-Rivers 1983.
1983A327.

279
Tanged knife with straight blade and thickened
convex back; rectangular section tang tapering to a
chisel end. Tang separated from blade by a raised
collar; slight barbs on tang. Traces of incised line
decoration on back of blade.
Lake Neuchatel.
L. 19.2 cm.
Purchased Pitt-Rivers 1983.
1983A328.

280
Tanged knife with slightly concave cutting edge
and thickened convex back.
Swiss Lakes, no provenance.
L. 17.9 cm.
Purchased Birmingham University Medical School
1973 (DCCCXLVIII).
1973A310.

281
Tanged knife with straight cutting edge curving up
at tip; back of blade straight and thickened. Square
section tang tapering to a chisel end; tang separated
from blade by a raised collar. Slightly curved bone
handle with notch and perforation at end.
Lake Neuchatel.
L. 27.9 cm.
Purchased Pitt-Rivers 1983.
1983A336.

282
Knife with straight back and cutting edge curving
to a point. Bronze handle cast on separately with
notch and perforation at end; separated from blade
by a raised collar.
Swiss Lakes, no provenance.
L. 29.2 cm.
Purchased Pitt-Rivers 1983.
1983A337.

283
Pegged, socketed, single-edged knife.
Lake Neuchatel.
L. 13.7 cm.
Purchased Pitt-Rivers 1983.
1983A325.

284
Concavo-convex razor with short, plain tang.
Lake Neuchatel.
L. 8.4 cm., W. 3.3 cm.
Purchased Pitt-Rivers 1983.
1983A244.

285
Concavo-convex razor with flat, circular perforated
tang.
Lake Neuchatel.
L. 8.9 cm., W. 3.0 cm.
Purchased Pitt-Rivers 1983.
1983A243.

286
Concavo-convex razor with flat circular tang.
Lake Neuchatel.
L. 7.1 cm., W. 2.0 cm.
Purchased Pitt-Rivers 1983.
1983A246.

287
Concavo-convex razor with flat rectangular
perforated tang.
Lake Neuchatel.
L. 8.6 cm., W. 2.0 cm.
Purchased Pitt-Rivers 1983.
1983A245.

288
Square ended tweezers made from bronze strip.
Swiss Lakes, no provenance.
L. 4.3 cm.
Purchased Pitt-Rivers 1983.
1983A248.

289
Fragmentary tweezers; ends missing.
Lake Neuchatel, Font.
extant L. 3.4 cm.
Purchased Pitt-Rivers 1983 ex Lawrence 1899.
1983A249.

290–299
Fish hooks with a single barb and curled tang.

290
Swiss Lakes, no provenance.
L. 5.6 cm.
Purchased Sandy 1948.
1948A161.

291
Swiss Lakes, no provenance.
L. 4.1 cm.
Purchased Pitt-Rivers 1983.
1983A222.

292
Swiss Lakes, no provenance.
L. 2.8 cm.
Purchased Pitt-Rivers 1983.
1983A224.

293
Swiss Lakes, no provenance.
L. 8.0 cm.
Purchased Pitt-Rivers 1983.
1983A1059.

294
Lake Neuchatel.
L. 4.7 cm.
Purchased Pitt-Rivers 1983 ex Roots.
Christies 20/04/1891.
1983A220.

295
Lake Neuchatel.
L. 4.6 cm.
Purchased Pitt-Rivers 1983 ex Roots.
Christies 20/04/1891.
1983A225.

296
Larger heavy fish hook made from square section
rod and with grooves in back of tang.
Lake Neuchatel.
L. 8.0 cm.
Purchased Pitt-Rivers 1983.
1983A236.

297
Lake Neuchatel, Font.
L. 5.6 cm.
Purchased Pitt-Rivers 1983 ex Lawrence April 1899.
1983A226.

298
Lake Bienne, Locraz.
L. 3.2 cm.
Purchased Pitt-Rivers 1983 ex Lawrence 1898.
1983A221.

299
Lake Bienne, Locraz.
L. 5.4 cm.
Purchased Pitt-Rivers 1983 ex Lawrence 1898.
1983A235.

300–305
Fish hooks with single barb and tang curled over
in opposite plain to hook.

300
Swiss Lakes, no provenance.
L. 5.2 cm.
Purchased 1983 Pitt-Rivers.
1983A1060.

301
Lake Neuchatel.
L. 4.2 cm.
Purchased 1951 Worcester Museum.
1951A723.

302
Lake Neuchatel.
L. 5.0 cm.
Purchased 1951 Worcester Museum.
1951A724.

303
Lake Neuchatel.
L. 4.3 cm.
Purchased 1983 Pitt-Rivers.
1983A230.

304
Lake Bienne, Locraz.
L. 2.9 cm.
Purchased Pitt-Rivers 1983 ex Lawrence 1898.
1983A229.

305
Lake Bienne, Locraz.
L. 5.4 cm.
Purchased Pitt-Rivers 1983 ex Lawrence 1898.
1983A233.

306–312
Fish hooks with single barb and notched tang.

306
Swiss Lakes, no provenance.
L. 3.5 cm.
Purchased Pitt-Rivers 1983.
1983A228.

307
Swiss Lakes, no provenance.
L. 5.0 cm.
Purchased Pitt-Rivers 1983.
1983A219.

Switzerland

308
Swiss Lakes, no provenance.
L. 4.0 cm.
Purchased Pitt-Rivers 1983.
1983A231.

309
Lake Neuchatel, Font.
L. 5.0 cm.
Purchased Pitt-Rivers 1983 ex Lawrence April 1899.
1983A232.

310
Lake Bienne, Locraz.
L. 3.3 cm.
Purchased Pitt-Rivers 1983 ex Lawrence 1898.
1983A227.

311
Lake Bienne, Locraz.
L. 3.4 cm.
Purchased Pitt-Rivers 1983.
1983A217.

312
Incised encircling lines all round rod.
Lake Bienne, Locraz.
L. 7.5 cm.
Purchased Pitt-Rivers 1983 ex Lawrence 1898.
1983A234.

313
Fish hook with single barb and straight plain tang.
Lake Bienne, Locraz.
L. 3.6 cm.
Purchased Pitt-Rivers 1983 ex Lawrence 1898.
1983A218.

314–316
Fish hooks with single barb and plain straight
flattened tang.

314
Swiss Lakes, no provenance.
L. 4.5 cm.
Purchased Pitt-Rivers 1983.
1983A1061.

315
Lake Neuchatel.
L. 4.0 cm.
Purchased Pitt-Rivers 1983 ex Lawrence 1898.
1983A216.

316
Lake Neuchatel.
L. 4.7 cm.
Purchased Pitt-Rivers 1983.
1983A223.

317
Large fish hook of rectangular section with single
barb formed by cutting a notch in hooked end;
straight tang.
Lake Neuchatel.
L. 7.5 cm.
Purchased Pitt-Rivers 1983.
1983A215.

318
Double fish hook.
Lake Bienne, Locraz.
L. 2.7 cm.
Purchased Pitt-Rivers 1983 ex Lawrence 1898.
1983A237.

319
Double fish hook with tall loop.
Lake Neuchatel, Font.
L. 5.8 cm.
Purchased Pitt-Rivers 1983 ex Lawrence April 1899.
1983A240.

320
Double fish hook with no barbs.
Swiss Lakes, no provenance.
L. 1.6 cm.
Purchased Pitt-Rivers 1983.
1983A238.

321
Double fish hook with no barbs.
Lake Bienne, Locraz.
L. 1.7 cm.
Purchased Pitt-Rivers 1983 ex Lawrence 1898.
1983A239.

322
Small harpoon made from rectangular section rod
tapering to a point with single barb; tang end
broken.
Lake Neuchatel, Cortaillod.
L. 6.2 cm.
Purchased Pitt-Rivers 1983.
1983A1062.

323
Length of wire bent over at each end and crossed
to form a loop in centre; fish hook?
Swiss Lakes, no provenance.
L. 5.2 cm.
Purchased Pitt-Rivers 1983.
1983A453.

324
Pegged socketed spearhead with long slender leaf
shaped blade; central rib down both faces formed
by continuation of socket. Blow holes in rib and
near top of socket.
Lake Neuchatel.
L. 22.7 cm., blade W. 4.7 cm., di. socket at mouth
2.0 cm.
Purchased Pitt-Rivers 1983.
1983A356.

325
Pegged socketed spearhead with leaf shaped blade
and central rib on each face formed by
continuation of socket.
Swiss Lakes, no provenance.
L. 12.2 cm., blade W. 3.2 cm., di. socket at mouth
2.2 cm.
Purchased Pitt-Rivers 1983 ex Roots collection.
Christies 20/04/1891.
1983A355.

326
Tanged arrowhead with slender leaf shaped blade
with slight midrib. Rectangular section tang
tapering to a chisel end.
Lake Neuchatel.
L. 6.1 cm.
Purchased Pitt-Rivers 1983.
1983A340.

327
Tanged arrowhead with triangular blade and long
pointed tang.
Lake Neuchatel.
L. 5.1 cm.
Purchased Pitt-Rivers 1983.
1983A353.

328
Barbed and tanged arrowhead with midrib; long
pointed tang.
Swiss Lakes, no provenance.
L. 4.0 cm.
Purchased Pitt-Rivers 1983.
1983A351.

329
Barbed and tanged arrowhead; long pointed tang.
Lake Neuchatel.
L. 4.4 cm.
Purchased Pitt-Rivers 1983.
1983A352.

330
Barbed and tanged arrowhead with midrib; tang
broken off.
Swiss Lakes, no provenance.
L. 3.9 cm.
Purchased Pitt-Rivers 1983.
1983A354.

331
Pin with conical head.
Swiss Lakes, no provenance.
L. 5.2 cm.
Purchased Pitt-Rivers 1983.
1983A313.

332
Pin with conical head; top of shank decorated with
incised lines.
Swiss Lakes, no provenance.
L. 17.1 cm.
Purchased Pitt-Rivers 1983.
1983A318.

333
Pin with biconical head decorated with three
groups of incised concentric circles; top of shank
decorated with incised encircling lines and two
bands of chevrons.
Lake Neuchatel.
L. 9.6 cm.
Purchased Worcester Museum 1951.
1951A612.
Note that decoration is very unusual on this type
c.f. Audouze and Courtois 1970, type H discussion.

334
Pin with biconical head.
Lake Neuchatel.
L. 14.3 cm.
Purchased Worcester Museum 1951.
1951A617.

335
Pin with biconical head.
Swiss Lakes, no provenance.
L. 8.7 cm.
Purchased Pitt-Rivers 1983.
1983A291.

336
Pin with biconical head.
Swiss Lakes, no provenance.
L. 6.7 cm.
Purchased Pitt-Rivers 1983.
1983A294.

337
Pin with biconical head; traces of concentric circle
decoration on top of head.
Lake Neuchatel.
L. 12.5 cm.
Purchased Pitt-Rivers 1983.
1983A295.

338
Pin with biconical head.
Lake Neuchatel.
L. 11 cm.
Purchased Pitt-Rivers 1983.
1983A296.

339
Pin with biconical head decorated with vertical
lines along carination. Top of shank decorated with
incised encircling lines.
Lake Neuchatel.
L. 12.7 cm.
Purchased Pitt-Rivers 1983.
1983A297.

340
Pin with biconical head.
Lake Neuchatel, Font.
L. 7.4 cm.
Purchased Pitt-Rivers 1983 ex Lawrence March
1899.
1983A298.

341
Pin with biconical head decorated with encircling
lines.
Lake Neuchatel.
L. 12.2 cm.
Purchased Pitt-Rivers 1983 ex Mr. Henry Castlemay
(December 1893?).
1983A300.

342
Pin with biconical head decorated with concentric
circles.
Swiss Lakes, no provenance.
L. 12.7 cm.
Purchased Pitt-Rivers 1983.
1983A301.

343
Pin with biconical head decorated with concentric
circles.
Lake Neuchatel.
L. 12.9 cm.
Purchased Pitt-Rivers 1983.
1983A302.

344
Pin with biconical head.
Swiss Lakes, no provenance.
L. 7.7 cm.
Purchased Pitt-Rivers 1983.
1983A308.

Switzerland

345
Pin with heavy biconical head.
Swiss Lakes, no provenance.
L. 9.9 cm.
Purchased Pitt-Rivers 1983.
1983A309.

346
Pin with biconical head.
Lake Neuchatel, Font.
L. 12.5 cm.
Purchased Pitt-Rivers 1983 ex Lawrence March 1899.
1983A312.

347
Pin with biconical head.
Swiss Lakes, no provenance.
L. 18.9 cm.
Purchased Pitt-Rivers 1983.
1983A316.

348
Pin with biconical head.
Swiss Lakes, no provenance.
L. 16.4 cm.
Purchased Pitt-Rivers 1983.
1983A319.

349
Pin with biconical head decorated with incised concentric circles.
Swiss Lakes, no provenance.
L. 15.1 cm.
Purchased Pitt-Rivers 1983.
1983A1034.

350
Pin with biconical head.
Swiss Lakes, no provenance.
L. 18.7 cm.
Purchased Pitt-Rivers 1983.
1983A1035.

351
Pin with biconical head; upper part of shank decorated with incised lines.
Swiss Lakes, no provenance.
L. 21.0 cm.
Purchased Pitt-Rivers 1983.
1983A1036.

352
Pin with hemispherical head; lower part of shank rectangular in section.
Swiss Lakes, no provenance.
L. 13.4 cm.
Purchased Pitt-Rivers 1983.
1983A310.

353
Pin with cylindro-conical head; cylinder decorated with incised encircling lines bordered by a band of short oblique slashes at top and bottom.
Swiss Lakes, no provenance.
L. 6.6 cm.
Purchased Pitt-Rivers 1983.
1983A293.

354
Pin with cylindro-conical head; wide groove around cylinder.
Swiss Lakes, no provenance.
L. 13.8 cm.
Purchased Pitt-Rivers 1983.
1983A315.

355
Pin with very crude cylindro-conical head; sides of cylinder flattened in places. Top of shank decorated with incised encircling lines.
Lake Bienne, Locraz.
L. 5.0 cm.
Purchased Pitt-Rivers 1983 ex Lawrence 1898.
1983A306.

356
Pin with cylindro-conical head; cylinder flattened off to produce polygonal sides. Incised concentric circles on top and bottom of head. Point broken off.
Lake Neuchatel, Font.
extant L. 11.1 cm.
Purchased Pitt-Rivers 1983 ex Lawrence March 1899.
1983A314.

357
Pin with heavy biconvex, almost lentoid, head; narrow shank.
Lake Neuchatel, Font.
L. 5.8 cm.
Purchased Pitt-Rivers 1983 ex Lawrence March 1899.
1983A288.

358
Pin with plain, very diminutive spherical head.
Lake Neuchatel.
L. 13.7 cm.
Purchased Worcester Museum 1951.
1951A613.

359
Pin with spherical head.
Swiss Lakes, no provenance.
L. 9.2 cm.
Purchased Pitt-Rivers 1983.
1983A289.

360
Very short pin with spherical head.
Swiss Lakes, no provenance.
L. 2.7 cm.
Purchased Pitt-Rivers 1983.
1983A290.

361
Pin with spherical head.
Lake Neuchatel.
L. 12.6 cm.
Purchased Pitt-Rivers 1983.
1983A292.

362
Pin with spherical head.
Lake Neuchatel?
L. 6.8 cm.
Purchased Pitt-Rivers 1983.
1983A303.

Switzerland

363
Pin with spherical head.
Lake Neuchatel, Font.
L. 6.4 cm.
Purchased Pitt-Rivers 1983 ex Lawrence March 1899.
1983A304.

364
Pin with large, heavy spherical head on thin shank.
Swiss Lakes, no provenance.
L. 6.3 cm.
Purchased Pitt-Rivers 1983.
1983A305.

365
Pin with spherical head decorated with incised concentric circles top and bottom.
Swiss Lakes, no provenance.
L. 11.5 cm.
Purchased Pitt-Rivers 1983.
1983A311.

366
Pin with spherical head.
Swiss Lakes, no provenance.
L. 8.2 cm.
Purchased Pitt-Rivers 1983.
1983A1049.

367
Hollow, spherical-headed pin with three holes; traces of concentric circle decoration at base where shank joins.
Swiss Lakes, no provenance.
L. 13.1 cm.
Purchased Sandy, 1948.
1948A98.

368
Hollow, spherical-headed pin with three holes; almost triangular in plan. Traces of line decoration on underside of head.
Swiss Lakes, no provenance.
L. 13.3 cm.
Purchased Pitt-Rivers 1983.
1983A1032.

369
Hollow, spherical-headed pin with four holes, each decorated with a ring of punched dots. Top and base of head decorated with incised concentric circles and ring of punched dots. Top of shank with horizontal ribs.
Lake Neuchatel.
L. 22.0 cm.
Acquisition details unknown.
1954A23.

370
Hollow, spherical-headed pin with four holes; each hole and top and base of head decorated with incised concentric circles. Shank projects very slightly from top of head.
Swiss Lakes, no provenance.
L. 20.0 cm.
Purchased Blackmore 1968.
1968A1987.

371
Hollow, spherical-headed pin with four holes; each hole and top and base of head decorated with

concentric circles. Wire coiled around top of shank.
Swiss Lakes, no provenance.
L. 20.7 cm.
Purchased Pitt-Rivers 1983.
1983A323.

372
Hollow, spherical-headed pin with four holes; each hole and top and base of head decorated with incised concentric circles. Metal ribbon coiled around top of shank.
Swiss Lakes, no provenance.
L. 17.5 cm.
Purchased Pitt-Rivers 1983.
1983A324.

373
Hollow, spherical-headed pin with six holes arranged in two rows; each hole and top and base of head decorated with concentric circles and ring of punched dots connected by bands of parallel lines.
Swiss Lakes, no provenance.
L. 24.5 cm.
Purchased Pitt-Rivers 1983.
1983A1031.

374
Roll topped pin.
Lake Neuchatel.
L. 10.6 cm.
Purchased Worcester Museum 1951.
1951A609.

375
Roll topped pin with two bronze rings linked by a strip of sheet bronze attached to head.
Swiss Lakes, no provenance.
L. 8.8 cm., di. rings 2.3 and 2.2 cm.
Purchased Pitt-Rivers 1983.
1983A254.

376
Roll topped pin with ring attached through head.
Swiss Lakes, no provenance.
L. 11.9 cm., di. ring 2.1 cm.
Purchased Pitt-Rivers 1983.
1983A255.

377
Roll topped pin with ring attached through head.
Swiss Lakes, no provenance.
L. 7.7 cm., di. ring 1.8 cm.
Purchased Pitt-Rivers 1983.
1983A256.

378
Roll topped pin with ring attached through head.
Swiss Lakes, no provenance.
L. 6.8 cm., di. ring 1.9 cm.
Purchased Pitt-Rivers 1983.
1983A257.

379
Small roll topped pin with ring attached through head.
Swiss Lakes, no provenance.
L. 3.0 cm., di. ring 2.0 cm.
Purchased Pitt-Rivers 1983.
1983A258.

380
Roll topped pin.
Swiss Lakes, no provenance.
L. 10.9 cm.
Purchased Pitt-Rivers 1983.
1983A259.

381
Roll topped pin.
Swiss Lakes, no provenance.
L. 12.5 cm.
Purchased Pitt-Rivers 1983.
1983A261.

382
Roll topped pin.
Swiss Lakes, no provenance.
L. 7.9 cm.
Purchased Pitt-Rivers 1983.
1983A262.

383
Roll topped pin.
Swiss Lakes, no provenance.
L. 9.9 cm.
Purchased Pitt-Rivers 1983.
1983A263.

384
Roll topped pin with spiral ribbing on shank; tip
missing.
Swiss Lakes, no provenance.
L. 7.9 cm.
Purchased Pitt-Rivers 1983.
1983A264.

385
Roll topped pin.
Swiss Lakes, no provenance.
L. 7.8 cm.
Purchased Pitt-Rivers 1983.
1983A265.

386
Roll topped pin.
Swiss Lakes, no provenance.
L. 9.3 cm.
Purchased Pitt-Rivers 1983.
1983A266.

387
Roll topped pin.
Swiss Lakes, no provenance.
L. 11.8 cm.
Purchased Pitt-Rivers 1983.
1983A267.

388
Roll topped pin.
Swiss Lakes, no provenance.
L. 11.4 cm.
Purchased Pitt-Rivers 1983.
1983A268.

389
Roll topped pin; square cross section.
Swiss Lakes, no provenance.
L. 8.6 cm.
Purchased Pitt-Rivers 1983.
1983A269.

390
Roll topped pin.
Swiss Lakes, no provenance.
L. 14.1 cm.
Purchased Pitt-Rivers 1983.
1983A270.

391
Small roll topped pin with spiral ribbing on shank.
Swiss Lakes, no provenance.
L. 4.0 cm.
Purchased Pitt-Rivers 1983.
1983A271.

392
Small roll topped pin.
Swiss Lakes, no provenance.
L. 4.6 cm.
Purchased Pitt-Rivers 1983.
1983A272.

393
Roll topped pin.
Swiss Lakes, no provenance.
L. 12.0 cm.
Purchased Pitt-Rivers 1983.
1983A1044.

394
Roll topped pin.
Swiss Lakes, no provenance.
L. 11.0 cm.
Purchased Pitt-Rivers 1983.
1983A1045.

395
Roll topped pin.
Swiss Lakes, no provenance.
L. 9.4 cm.
Purchased Pitt-Rivers 1983.
1983A1046.

396
Roll topped pin.
Swiss Lakes, no provenance.
L. 8.1 cm.
Purchased Pitt-Rivers 1983.
1983A1047.

397
Roll topped pin.
Swiss Lakes, no provenance.
L. 8.0 cm.
Purchased Pitt-Rivers 1983.
1983A1048.

398
Vase headed pin with traces of ribbing at top of
shank.
Swiss Lakes, no provenance.
L. 15.6 cm.
Purchased Pitt-Rivers 1983.
1983A279.

399
Vase headed pin with convex top; ribbing on top of
shank.
Swiss Lakes, no provenance.
L. 17.2 cm.
Purchased Pitt-Rivers 1983.
1983A283.

400
Vase headed pin with convex top; ribbing at top of shank.
Lake Neuchatel, Font.
L. 15.3 cm.
Purchased Pitt-Rivers 1983 ex Lawrence April 1899.
1983A282.

401
Vase headed pin with convex top; ribbing at top of shank.
Swiss Lakes, no provenance.
L. 12.8 cm.
Purchased Pitt-Rivers 1983.
1983A280.

402
Vase headed pin with convex top.
Swiss Lakes, no provenance.
L. 16.3 cm.
Purchased Pitt-Rivers 1983.
1983A278.

403
Vase headed pin with flat top.
Lake Neuchatel.
L. 18.2 cm.
Purchased Worcester Museum 1951.
1951A618.

404
Vase headed pin with flat top.
Lake Neuchatel, Font.
L. 12.4 cm.
Purchased Pitt-Rivers 1983 ex Lawrence March 1899.
1983A281.

405
Vase headed pin with flat top.
Lake Neuchatel.
L. 7.9 cm.
Purchased Worcester Museum 1951.
1951A611.

406
Vase headed pin with flat top decorated with two incised concentric circles. Traces of incised encircling lines on top of shank.
Lake Neuchatel.
L. 19.9 cm.
Purchased Worcester Museum 1951.
1951A614.

407
Vase headed pin with flat top; ribbing at top of shank.
Swiss Lakes, no provenance.
L. 18.2 cm.
Purchased Pitt-Rivers 1983.
1983A287.

408
Vase headed pin with slightly conical projecting top decorated with concentric circles; ribbing at top of shank.
Swiss Lakes, no provenance.
L. 17.5 cm.
Purchased Pitt-Rivers 1983.
1983A286.

409
Vase headed pin with flat projecting top decorated with concentric circles; ribbing at top of shank.
Swiss Lakes, no provenance.
L. 10.3 cm.
Purchased Pitt-Rivers 1983.
1983A273.

410
Vase headed pin with flat projecting top decorated with concentric circles; fine ribbing on top of shank.
Swiss Lakes, no provenance.
L. 9.9 cm.
Purchased Pitt-Rivers 1983.
1983A275.

411
Vase headed pin with flat projecting top decorated with concentric circles; ribbing on top of shank.
Swiss Lakes, no provenance.
L. 16.6 cm.
Purchased Pitt-Rivers 1983.
1983A285.

412
Vase headed pin with flat projecting top.
Swiss Lakes, no provenance.
L. 9.2 cm.
Purchased Pitt-Rivers 1983.
1983A276.

413
Vase headed pin with flat projecting top decorated with concentric circles.
Swiss Lakes, no provenance.
L. 20.9 cm.
Purchased Pitt-Rivers 1983.
1983A284.

414
Vase headed pin with flat top; three bands of incised line decoration on upper shank.
Swiss Lakes, no provenance.
L. 14.1 cm.
Purchased Pitt-Rivers 1983.
1983A1037.

415
Vase headed pin with flat top.
Swiss Lakes, no provenance.
L. 14.4 cm.
Purchased Pitt-Rivers 1983.
1983A1038.

416
Vase headed pin with flat top.
Swiss Lakes, no provenance.
L. 17.7 cm.
Purchased Pitt-Rivers 1983.
1983A1039.

417
Vase headed pin with flat top; fine ribbing on top of shank.
Swiss Lakes, no provenance.
L. 16.5 cm.
Purchased Pitt-Rivers 1983.
1983A1040.

418
Vase headed pin with flat top.

Swiss Lakes, no provenance.
L. 18.4 cm.
Purchased Pitt-Rivers 1983.
1983A1041.

419
Pin with separately attached disc top; ribbing on top of shank.
Swiss Lakes, no provenance [Lac du Bourget?].
L. 9.6 cm.
Purchased Pitt-Rivers 1983.
1983A274.
This type is peculiar to Lac du Bourget sites c.f. Audouze and Courtois 1970, type Q sub type 8.

420
Pin with spherical head and two widely spaced lentoid swellings below; decorated with incised encircling lines.
Swiss Lakes, no provenance.
L. 20.0 cm.
Purchased Pitt-Rivers 1983.
1983A317.

421
Pin with spherical head and two widely spaced lentoid swellings below; decorated with fine spiral ribbing. The shank below the lowest swelling has a thin ribbon of sheet metal coiled around it.
Swiss Lakes, no provenance.
L. 23.2 cm.
Purchased Pitt-Rivers 1983.
1983A321.

422
Pin with biconical head and two widely spaced lentoid swellings below; decorated with spiral ribbing.
Swiss Lakes, no provenance.
L. 25.9 cm.
Purchased Pitt-Rivers 1983.
1983A320.

423
Pin with roughly spherical head and two widely spaced lentoid swellings below; decorated with spiral incised line.
Swiss Lakes, no provenance.
L. 17.1 cm.
Purchased Pitt-Rivers 1983.
1983A1033.

424
Pin with flat nail head.
Swiss Lakes, no provenance.
L. 15.5 cm.
Purchased Pitt-Rivers 1983.
1983A1042.

425
Pin with flattened spherical head; possibly derived from poppy-headed type.
Swiss Lakes, no provenance.
L. 7.6 cm.
Purchased Pitt-Rivers 1983.
1983A299.

426
Pin with heavy convex head and moulding below; ribbon coiled around shank.
Swiss Lakes, no provenance.
L. 12.4 cm.

Purchased Pitt-Rivers 1983.
1983A322.

427
Pin with stepped nail head.
Swiss Lakes, no provenance.
L. 5.5 cm.
Purchased Pitt-Rivers 1983.
1983A307.

428
Pin with biconical head, flattened on top.
Swiss Lakes, no provenance.
L. 8.7 cm.
Purchased Sandy 1948.
1948A99.

429
Dish-headed pin with two raised bands at top of shank.
Swiss Lakes, no provenance.
L. 11.1 cm.
Purchased Sandy 1948.
1948A100.

430
Pin made from plain circular section rod the top of which has been bent over to form a loop to which is attached a chain of four rings connected to each other by strips of sheet bronze.
Swiss Lakes, no provenance.
L. 7.9 cm., di. rings 1.3, 1.2, 1.3, 1.2 cm.
Purchased Pitt-Rivers 1983.
1983A253.

431
Pin flattened at head end and bent over into a squashed shepherd's crook; end split into two strands.
Swiss Lakes, no provenance.
L. 13.3 cm.
Purchased Pitt-Rivers 1983.
1983A260.

432
Pin with spiral ribbing along most of shank; head broken off but flattened towards this end therefore possibly roll topped?
Lake Neuchatel.
extant L. 9.6 cm.
Purchased Worcester Museum 1951.
1951A616.
C.f. possibly also Audouze and Courtois 1970, 279, 280 (twisted shank).

433
Pin with flat nail head and raised mouldings below; possibly separately attached to shank.
Swiss Lakes, no provenance.
L. 13.6 cm.
Purchased Pitt-Rivers 1983.
1983A277.

434
Head only from a pin; cylindro-conical with groove in side of cylinder and knob on top of cone.
Swiss Lakes, no provenance.
extant L. 1.8 cm.
Purchased Pitt-Rivers 1983.
1983A450.

Switzerland

435
Plain, simple fibula.
Swiss Lakes, no provenance.
L. 9.4 cm.
Purchased Pitt-Rivers 1983.
1983A347.

436
Iron fibula fragment with three coils either side of
bow.
Lake Neuchatel.
L. 6.1 cm., W. 2.2 cm.
Purchased Worcester Museum 1951.
1951A606.

437
Iron fibula fragment with six coils either side of
bow.
Lake Neuchatel.
L. 7.8 cm., W. 4.8 cm.
Purchased Worcester Museum 1951.
1961A605.

438
Wide armlet with crescentic section and out-turned
terminals. Decorated with groups of incised lines,
concentric ovals and half circles.
Lake Neuchatel, St. Blaise.
max. di. 10.1 cm., H. 3.0 cm.
Purchased Pitt-Rivers 1983.
1983A400.

439
Wide armlet with crescentic section and out-turned
terminals. Decorated with groups of incised lines,
concentric circles and half circles now quite feint
in places.
Swiss Lakes, no provenance.
max. di. 10.4 cm., H. 3.2 cm.
Purchased Pitt-Rivers 1983.
1983A399.

440
Hollow cast penannular bracelet with flattened, out-
turned terminals. Decorated with parallel lines
giving a crude ribbed appearance. Badly cast and
many air bubbles visible.
Lake Neuchatel, Auvernier.
max. di. 7.5 cm.
Purchased Pitt-Rivers 1983.
1983A401.

441
Penannular earring decorated with five raised ribs.
Lake Neuchatel.
Di. 1.6 cm.
Purchased Pitt-Rivers 1983 ex lawrence 1898.
1983A437.

442
Penannular earring deocrated with five raised ribs;
one end broken.
Lake Neuchatel.
Di. 1.7 cm.
Purchased Pitt-Rivers 1983 ex Lawrence 1898.
1983A438.

443
Penannular earring decorated with five raised ribs.
Swiss Lakes, no provenance.
Di. 1.8 cm.
Purchased Pitt-Rivers 1983.

1983A439.

444
Penannular earring decorated with three incised
lines; pointed tapering terminals overlap.
Lake Neuchatel.
Di. 1.7 cm.
Purchased Pitt-Rivers 1983.
1983A440.

445
Fragment of earring decorated with four incised
lines.
Swiss Lakes, no provenance.
Di. 1.3 cm.
Purchased Pitt-Rivers 1983.
1983A441.

446
Heavy, circular bronze bead of uneven height.
Swiss Lakes, no provenance.
Di. 1.8 cm., max. H. 1.4 cm.
Purchased Pitt-Rivers 1983.
1983A442.

447
Double spiral pendant.
Lake Neuchatel, Font.
max. W. 4.4 cm.
Purchased Pitt-Rivers 1983 ex Lawrence April 1899.
1983A417.

448
Flat, open-cast, triangular pendant with circular
suspension loop; decorated with incised lines and
hatching.
Lake Neuchatel.
H. 6.0 cm., max. W. 2.7 cm.
Purchased Pitt-Rivers 1983.
1983A419.

449
Flat, open-cast, triangular pendant with circular
suspension loop; decorated with incised lines and
hatching.
Swiss Lakes, no provenance.
H. 6.1 cm., max. W. 3.0 cm.
Purchased Pitt-Rivers 1983.
1983A418.

450
Flat pendant in the form of a ring with projecting
suspension loop; undecorated.
Lake Neuchatel.
Di. 4.0 cm.
Purchased Pitt-Rivers 1983.
1983A422.

451
Ring pendant with projecting suspension loop; solid
triangular section. Decorated with incised lines.
Lake Neuchatel.
Di. 3.6 cm.
Purchased Pitt-Rivers 1983.
1983A421.

452
Pendant with serrated edges ending in a fish-tail
shape at one end and a suspension loop at the
other. Attached to an open ring.
Lake Neuchatel.
L. 4.9 cm., di. ring 3.5 cm.

Purchased Pitt-Rivers 1983.
1983A1054.

453
Pendant in the form of a closed ring with two
straight horn-like projections.
Lake Neuchatel, Font.
W. 2.9 cm.
Purchased Pitt-Rivers 1983 ex Lawrence 1899.
1983A1056.

454
Slightly convex circular boss with projecting
rectangular attachment loop on reverse; face plain.
The loop is off centre and it is possible that the
piece has been cut down.
Swiss Lakes, no provenance.
Di. 3.4 cm.
Purchased Pitt-Rivers 1983.
1983A406.

455
Plain, slightly convex circular disc with projecting
attachment loop on reverse; loop is off centre.
Lake Neuchatel, Font.
Di. 4.3 cm.
Purchased Pitt-Rivers 1983 ex Lawrence April 1899.
1983A413.

456
Plain conical disc with attachment loop on concave
reverse.
Lake Neuchatel.
Di. 3.2 cm.
Purchased Pitt-Rivers 1983 ex Lawrence 1898.
1983A414.

457
Plain conical disc with attachment loop on concave
reverse.
Lake Neuchatel, St. Blaise.
Di. 3.1 cm.
Purchased Pitt-Rivers 1983.
1983A412.

458
Circular domed boss with attachment loop on
concave reverse.
Lake Neuchatel.
Di. 2.4 cm.
Purchased Pitt-Rivers 1983.
1983A410.

459
Circular domed boss with attachment loop on
concave reverse.
Swiss Lakes, no provenance.
Di. 2.3 cm.
Purchased Pitt-Rivers 1983.
1983A415.

460
Conical boss with rounded knob at centre and two
repoussé concentric circles around circumference.
Attachment loop on concave reverse.
Lake Neuchatel, Font.
Di. 3.6 cm.
Purchased Pitt-Rivers 1983 ex Lawrence April 1899.
1983A411.

461
Convex circular boss decorated with two repoussé
concentric circles round circumference. Attachment
loop on concave reverse.
Lake Neuchatel, Font.
Di. 3.5 cm.
Purchased Pitt-Rivers 1983 ex Lawrence April 1899.
1983A407.

462
Large, slightly convex circular boss; edge decorated
with repoussé dots and three concentric circles.
Rivet in centre to suspension loop on reverse.
Lake Neuchatel, St. Blaise.
Di. 8.5 cm.
Purchased Pitt-Rivers 1983.
1983A404.

463
Circular "cap" with two perforations through top.
Rim pierced by four pairs of rivets into remains of
leather.
Swiss Lakes, no provenance.
Di. 6.4 cm.
Purchased Pitt-Rivers 1983.
1983A405.

464
"Hat-shaped" piece consisting of a flat circular rim
with a rounded dome on top of which is a
suspension loop.
Swiss Lakes, no provenance.
Di. 4.2 cm., H. 1.7 cm.
Purchased Pitt-Rivers 1983.
1983A409.

465
A flat circular piece with a heavy perforated
projection with a bevelled rim from the centre.
Underside rough cast and presumably not intended
to be seen.
Swiss Lakes, no provenance.
Di. 3.2 cm., H. 1.6 cm.
Purchased Pitt-Rivers 1983.
1983A408.

466
Small flat circular button with attachment loop on
reverse.
Swiss Lakes, no provenance.
Di. 1.8 cm.
Purchased Pitt-Rivers 1983.
1983A448.

467
Convex circular button with attachment loop on
concave reverse.
Swiss Lakes, no provenance.
Di. 1.8 cm.
Purchased Pitt-Rivers 1983.
1983A452.

468
Steeply domed button with attachment loop on
reverse.
Swiss Lakes, no provenance.
Di. 1.3 cm.
Purchased Pitt-Rivers 1983.
1983A447.

469
Fastener in the shape of a bow tie with attachment
loop on reverse. See Munro 1890, 62 fig. 12 no. 9,
101 fig. 21 no. 33.

Swiss Lakes, no provenance.
W. 3.0 cm.
Purchased Pitt-Rivers 1983 ex Lawrence.
1983A416.

470
Cufflink-like stud with five-rayed star on head.
Swiss Lakes, no provenance.
H. 1.1 cm., max. di. 1.5 cm.
Purchased Pitt-Rivers 1983.
1983A1057.

471
Cufflink-like stud.
Swiss Lakes, no provenance.
H. 1.2 cm., di. 1.7 cm.
Purchased Pitt-Rivers 1983.
1983A451.

472
Fastener (buckle?) consisting of a flat circular stud
decorated with concentric circles attached to a
rectangular section shank which is bent at right
angles and ends in a ring. (See Keller 1878, pl. 122
nos. 1—5).
Swiss Lakes, no provenance.
H. 3.4 cm.
Purchased Pitt-Rivers 1983.
1983A444.

473
Belt or rein fitting consisting of a rectangular
piece of sheet metal bent over at each end to form
an open flattened loop. Incised line along each long
edge.
Swiss Lakes, no provenance.
L. 3.0 cm., H. 1.4 cm.
Purchased Pitt-Rivers 1983.
1983A443.

474
Fragment of chain formed of four rings connected
with strips of metal ribbon.
Swiss Lakes, no provenance.
L. 6.4 cm., di. rings 1.1, 1.1, 1.5, 1.1 cm.
Purchased Pitt-Rivers 1983.
1983A349.

475
Three closed rings attached to a fourth ring which
also has a spiral of bronze ribbon round part of it.
Lake Neuchatel, Font.
av. di. 2 cm.
Purchased Pitt-Rivers 1983 ex Lawrence April 1895!
1983A428.

476
Five closed cast rings attached to a sixth larger
ring partially wrapped with wire.
Swiss Lakes, no provenance.
one at di. 1.2 cm., four at 2.0 cm., one at 3.0 cm.
Purchased Pitt-Rivers 1983.
1983A429.

477
Two closed cast rings attached to a third partially
wrapped with ribbon.
Swiss Lakes, no provenance.
av. di. 2 cm.
Purchased Pitt-Rivers 1983.
1983A430.

478
Four closed cast rings of varying size attached to a
fifth partially wrapped with ribbon.
Lake Neuchatel, Font.
av. di. 1.5 cm.
Purchased Pitt-Rivers 1983 ex Lawrence April 1899.
1983A431

479
Two penannular rings and a loop attached to a
wire ring.
Lake Neuchatel.
di. 3.0 cm.
Purchased Worcester Museum 1951.
1951A622.

480
Penannular wire ring with pointed terminals.
Lake Neuchatel.
di. 2.6 cm.
Purchased Worcester Museum 1951.
1951A623.

481
Penannular wire ring; bent out of shape.
Lake Neuchatel.
di. 4.0 cm.
Purchased Worcester Museum 1951.
1951A624.

482
Penannular ring with flattened terminals;
misshapen.
Lake Neuchatel.
max. di. 3.0 cm.
Purchased Worcester Museum 1951.
1951A625.

483
Penannular wire ring; terminals broken and piece
misshapen.
Lake Neuchatel.
max. W. 2.5 cm.
Purchased Worcester Museum 1951.
1951A627.

484
Penannular wire ring.
Swiss Lakes, no provenance.
di. 3.0 cm.
Purchased Pitt-Rivers 1983.
1983A426.

485
Penannular wire ring.
Swiss Lakes, no provenance.
di. 2.7 cm.
Purchased Pitt-Rivers 1983.
1983A427.

486
Badly cast ring.
Lake Neuchatel.
di. 2.9 cm.
Purchased Worcester Museum 1951.
1951A619.

487
Badly cast ring.
Lake Neuchatel.
di. 2.9 cm.

Purchased Worcester Museum 1951.
1951A620.

488
Badly cast ring.
Lake Neuchatel.
di. 2.6 cm.
Purchased Worcester Museum 1951.
1951A621.

489
Two penannular rings with twisted spiral decoration
on one end and length of coiled ribbon over
opening. Smaller one has three small cast rings
attached to it and the larger one a single ring.
Lake Neuchatel, Estavayer.
di. 2.3cm., 3.0 cm.
Presented Wellcome Trustees 1982 (A191005).
Stevens 16–17/09/1930 lot 432.
1989A22.

490
Eight cast rings.
Lake Neuchatel, Font.
di. 2.0 to 4.3 cm.
Presented Wellcome Trustees 1982 (A191005).
Stevens 16–17/09/1930 lot 432.
1989A21.

491
Nineteen plain cast rings.
Lake Neuchatel.
di. 1.5 to 2.0 cm.
Purchased Pitt-Rivers 1983.
1983A433.

492
Twenty six plain cast rings.
Lake Bienne, Locraz.
av. di. 2 cm.
Purchased Pitt-Rivers 1983 ex Lawrence 1898.
1983A432.

493
About 140 plain cast rings.
Lake Neuchatel.
di. 1 to 3 cm.
Purchased Pitt-Rivers 1983 ex Lawrence 1898.
1983A434.

494
Penannular iron ring.
Lake Neuchatel.
di. 3.8 cm.
Purchased Worcester Museum 1951.
1951A607.

495
Iron ring.
Lake Neuchatel.
di. 2.9 cm.
Purchased Worcester Museum 1951.
1951A608.

496
Fragment of rectangular section rod broken at both
ends.
Lake Neuchatel.
extant L. 5.2 cm.
Purchased Worcester Museum 1951.
1951A615.

497
Length of bronze ribbon coiled into a spiral of six
and a half loops.
Lake Neuchatel, Font.
L. 2.9 cm., di. 1.5 cm.
Purchased Pitt-Rivers 1983 ex Lawrence 1899.
1983A1058.

498
Eight fragments of pin/needle shanks.
Swiss Lakes, no provenance.
L. 4.7 to 10.5 cm.
Purchased Pitt-Rivers 1983.
1983A1053.

499
Circular brooch comprising flattened ring with pin
attached by wrapping one end of bronze rod
around ring.
Swiss Lakes, no provenance.
Di. 2.7–2.9 cm.
Purchased Pitt-Rivers 1983.
1983A348.

500
Implement formed of circular section rod with
swollen rounded terminals at each end. Cosmetic
applicator or dropper? Roman?
Swiss Lakes, no provenance.
L. 15.5 cm.
Purchased Pitt-Rivers 1983.
1983A1043.

501
Implement formed from square section rod
hammered at both ends into paddle-like spatulae
set at right angles to each other. Roman?
Swiss Lakes, no provenance.
L. 15.4 cm.
Purchased Pitt-Rivers 1983.
1983A343.

502
Flat crescent shaped piece with three notches in
convex edge.
Lake Neuchatel, Font.
L. 7.5 cm.
Purchased Pitt-Rivers 1983 ex Lawrence April 1899.
1983A435.

503
Fragment of buckle in shape of a truncated
diamond; half missing.
Lake Neuchatel, Font.
extant L. 2.8 cm., W. 2.9 cm.
Purchased Pitt-Rivers 1983.
1983A445.

504
Roughly oval-shaped buckle.
Lake Neuchatel, Font.
L. 2.5 cm., W. 2.2 cm.
Purchased Pitt-Rivers 1983 ex Lawrence April 1890!
1983A446.

505
Spoon with small, circular bowl. Roman?
Swiss Lakes, no provenance.
L. 12.0 cm., di. bowl 2.2 cm.
Purchased Pitt-Rivers 1983.
1983A344.

506
Implement with flattened spade-shaped end.
Swiss Lakes, no provenance.
L. 10.9 cm.
Purchased Pitt-Rivers 1983.
1983A342.

507
Ear pick with head hammered to flat disc and bent
at an angle to the shaft. Roman?
Swiss Lakes, no provenance.
L. 19.5 cm.
Purchased Pitt-Rivers 1983.
1983A341.

508
Thin sheet of bronze rounded at one end and
pierced by three irregular rivet holes or casting
flaws and a deep V-shaped notch; tapers towards
other end which is broken. Miscast dagger blade?
Lake Neuchatel.
L. 8.3 cm.
Purchased Pitt-Rivers 1983.
1983A420.

509
Hollow sheet metal tube.
Lake Neuchatel.
L. 12.6 cm.
Purchased Pitt-Rivers 1983.
1983A350.

510
Tube.
Lake Neuchatel.
L. 10.7 cm.
Purchased Worcester Museum 1951.
1951A721.

511
Length of flat ribbon bent into a U-shape and
curled over at each end.
Swiss Lakes, no provenance.
L. 3.4 cm.
Purchased Pitt-Rivers 1983.
1983A454.

512
Unevenly stepped stud or pin head? with lump of
concreted iron on underside.
Swiss Lakes, no provenance.
di. 1.6 cm.
Purchased Pitt-Rivers 1983.
1983A449.

513
Fragment of tube.
Swiss Lakes, no provenance.
L. 2.9 cm.
Purchased Pitt-Rivers 1983.
1983A436.

UNPROVENANCED EUROPE [514–553]

514
High-flanged looped palstave with central midrib
and broad expanded blade. Swallow hole behind
loop.
Europe, no provenance; possibly France.
L. 16.1 cm., blade W. 6.4 cm
Purchased Pitt Rivers 1983.
1983A813.

515
Palstave with straight-edged blade decorated with
eight raised ribs on one face and nine on the other.
The piece is unfinished and retains ragged casting
seams along both sides and the edge of the blade
which is unsharpened. Casting flash remains on the
butt.
Europe, no provenance.
L. 14.5 cm., blade W. 5.0 cm.
Acquisition details unknown.
1962A396.

516
Heavy centre-winged axe with slight stop ridge at
bottom of wings. Notch in butt for hafting dowel.
Europe, no provenance; possibly France.
L. 18.5 cm., blade W. 5.3 cm.
Purchased Pitt-Rivers 1983.
1983A814.

517
Socketed axe with side loop and thickened bevelled
rim below which is a raised band. On each face, at
the height of the loop, is a single raised nipple or
imitation rivet head. Two haft ribs inside socket.
Europe, no provenance; possibly France.
L. 14.5 cm., blade W. 5.4 cm.
Purchased Pitt Rivers 1983 ex Julien.
Sothebys 18/03/1886 lot 50.
1983A816.

518
Socketed axe with small side loop and thickened
mouth moulding with very small raised band below.
Europe, no provenance.
L. 12.9 cm., blade W. 4.2 cm.
Acquisition details unknown.
1987A348.

519
Fragment of looped socketed axe; upper part only
preserved. Thickened mouth moulding with raised
band below; looped. Poorly cast with many air
bubbles and one hole.
Europe, no provenance; possibly France.
extant L. 7.0 cm.
Purchased Pitt rivers 1983.
1983A817.

520
Socketed axe with rectangular socket and broad flat
blade.
Europe, no provenance.
L. 9.0 cm., blade W. 7.3 cm.
Acquisition details unknown.
1962A397.

521
Socketed gouge with slightly concave blade faces
and square section shaft. Socket mouth is flared
and circular with inverted rim; broken. Deliberate
deep V-shaped split in socket on one face only.
Probably a carpentry tool for cutting mortices.
Europe, no provenance; possibly British.
L. 12.2 cm.
Acquisition details not recorded but probably
purchased Sandy 1948.
1962A395.

522
Cylindrical macehead with tapering socket which
extends to the open tip. Body has seven raised

"fins" for most of its length. Single peg hole in socket. Shaft contains tapering length of wood - ancient?
Europe; marked "France, Italy or Balkans".
L. 19.5 cm., max. W. 4.2 cm.
Purchased Blackmore 1968.
1968A1499.

523
Shepherd's crook pin of circular section rod flattened to form the head.
Europe, no provenance.
L. 5.3 cm. (bent out of shape).
Acquisition details unknown.
1962A406.

524
Hat-topped pin with biconical swelling below. Shank square in section near head then circular. Tip broken off.
Europe, no provenance.
extant L. 19.1 cm.
Acquisition details unknown.
1948A233.2

525
Hat-topped pin with globular swelling below. Shank of circular section. Tip broken off.
Europe, no provenance.
extant L. 18.5 cm.
Acquisition details unknown.
1948A233.1

526
Small single-piece spectacle brooch consisting of two coils linked by a figure of eight. Alexander 1965, type Ib.
Europe, no exact provenance (see Alexander 1965, ill. 4 for distribution of this type).
W. 5.0 cm.
Purchased Sotheby's 1960.
Sotheby's 12/12/1960 lot 28.
1962A408.

527
Large multi-piece double spectacle brooch consisting of four coils. A separate back plate forms the catchpiece and pin, the tip of which is now missing. The ends of the four coils are riveted to the back plate with a single rivet and the junction disguised with a decorative sheet element, now damaged. Each coil has a domed central boss, one now missing; in two instances this is riveted to the back plate and in the other two through a sheet washer on the back of the coil. Alexander 1965, type IV.
Europe, no exact provenance; possibly Italy.
max. W. 17.9 cm.
Acquisition details unknown.
1964A2.

528
Bow brooch with tapering rectangular section; bow beaten to a rod to form a single coil spring and pin at one end and hammered flat and bent over to form a catch plate at the other. The catchplate is broken and part is adhering to the pin. Top of bow decorated with oblique line decoration.
No exact provenance; possibly Russia? or Baltic provinces?
max. W. 4.0 cm., H. 3.3 cm.
Presented Wellcome Trustees 1982 (R4668/1937).

Sotheby's 23/08/1930 lot 3.
1982A2400.

529
Fibula with tall ribbed foot and thick steeply arched bow. Spring and pin missing. Iberian type.
Europe, no provenance; possibly Spain?
L. 4.5 cm.
Purchased Pitt Rivers 1983.
1983A821.

530
Fibula with tall conical foot decorated with four notches; bow ribbed. Spring and pin missing. Iberian type. (See Hattatt 1987, no. 1366).
Europe, no provenance; possibly Spain?
L. 5.3 cm.
Purchased Pitt-Rivers 1983.
1983A820

531
Fibula with tall foot ending in a roughly square expanded terminal decorated with interlocking spirals. Bow decorated with lines and punched dots. Spring and pin missing. Iberian type.
Europe, no provenance; possibly Spain?
L. 6.1 cm.
Purchased Pitt Rivers 1983.
1983A819.

532
Fragment of fibula with tall foot with thick expanded terminal in shape of a concave-sided square; decorated with punched dots. Bow, spring and pin missing. Iberian type.
Europe, no provenance; possibly Spain?
L. 2.5 cm.
Purchased Pitt Rivers 1983.
1983A823.

533
Two fragments forming a complete chest ornament, belt or crown. It is made from circular section rod now bent out of shape and in places accidentally? coiled. The terminals are tapered and end in blunt points. The central section consists of three large flattened oval discs decorated with incised lines, punched dots and ring and dot motif; the design on the central disc differs slightly from that on the two outer ones.
Europe, no provenance; reputedly Switzerland.
centre disc 9.7 x 7.7 cm.
Presented F.C. Ohly 1962.
1962A401

534
Three fragments of bar twisted torque, one preserving a square section hooked terminal.
Europe, no provenance.
Longest fragment 15.8 cm.
Presented Wellcome Trustees 1982 (A200480).
1989A19

535
Penannular torque made from circular section rod tapering towards the flattened and coiled terminals. Undecorated.
Europe, no provenance; probably central.
max. external di. 15.1 cm.
Presented Clayton 1953.
1953A915.

536
Penannular torque made from circular section rod

with large, cupped, buffer terminals separately attached. Broken in two pieces.
Europe, no provenance; N. France or S. Britain.
max. external di. 13.5 cm.
Purchased 1960.
Sothebys 12/12/1960 lot 28.
1962A403.

537
Spiral armlet made from D-section rod and bent into 24 coils. Terminals plain, slightly tapered, with incised line decoration.
Central Europe.
overall L. 27 cm., external di. 6.0–9.0 cm.
Purchased Blackmore 1968.
1968A1316.

538
Three fragments probably from two bracelets. Crudely cast and of thick crescentic section. Decorated with lozenges between bands of vertical and horizontal lines.
Europe, no provenance.
Estimated di. 8.5 cm. and 10.5 cm.
Acquisition details unknown.
1962A404.

539
Bracelet of very flattened D-section with very feint traces of incised zig zag decoration. One terminal missing, other hammered into a rod and coiled up into a vertical spiral.
Central? Europe, no exact provenance.
max. Di. 6.0 cm.
Acquisition details unknown.
1963A902.

540
Fragment of penannular bracelet of thin flat section decorated with ribs and engraved decoration.
Europe, no provenance.
extant L. 2.5 cm.
Acquisition details unknown.
1962A407.

541
Penannular bracelet of flat section with deep horizontal ribbed decoration on the outside. Tapering towards the terminals which are broken off.
Europe, no provenance.
max. external di. 5.1 cm.
Purchased Blackmore 1968 (3 WB).
1968A1306.

542
Spiral bracelet of circular section rod flattened after one twist into a thin ribbon beyond which the piece is broken. The surviving terminal is thickened and decorated with grooves. The flattened section is decorated with two pairs of horizontal grooves between which is a row of widely spaced ring and dot motifs.
Northern Europe, no provenance.
max. external di. 9.3 cm.
Purchased Blackmore 1968 (57c).
1968A1309.

543
Penannular bracelet of circular section rod. The terminals are hammered flat and expanded into

large ovals decorated with punched dots and incised lines.
Western Europe, no provenance.
max. external di. 5.3 cm.
Acquisition details unknown.
1962A405.

544
Penannular bracelet of solid D-shaped section with slightly out-turned terminals. Decorated with nine groups of incised vertical lines arranged in three panels. Very similar to 202 above.
Europe, no provenance.
max. external di. 7.3 cm.
Purchased Blackmore 1968.
1968A1307.

545
Penannular bracelet of flattened D-shaped section which narrows to expanded terminals. The exterior is decorated with groups of diagonal lines with a diagonal cross near each terminal.
Europe, no provenance.
max. external di. 5.5 cm.
Purchased Blackmore 1968 (15 WB).
1968A1305.

546
Penannular hollow cast bracelet of circular section open along inside edge. Slightly expanded terminals with traces of a band of ladder motif decoration near each.
Europe, no provenance.
max. external di. 7.3 cm.
Purchased Blackmore 1968.
1968A1308.

547
Penannular bracelet of oval section. One terminal slightly expanded, the other broken. Decoration lost except for traces of chevrons.
Europe, no provenance.
max. external di. 6.2 cm.
Purchased Blackmore 1968 (15b).
1968A1310.

548
Spiral bracelet of circular section. Plain terminals each decorated with four bands of vertical ribs and a diagonal cross.
Europe, no provenance.
max. external di. 5.5 cm.
Purchased Sandy 1948.
1948A133.

549
Spiral bracelet of circular section rod. Plain terminals. Undecorated.
Europe, no provenance.
max. external di. 4.5 cm.
Purchased Blackmore 1968 (54a; 16; M21).
1968A1311.

550
Spiral bracelet of circular section. Plain terminals. Undecorated.
Europe, no provenance.
max. external di. 8.0 cm.
Acquisition details unknown.
1962A402.

551
Penannular earring made from tapering circular
section rod.
Europe, no provenance.
max. di. 2.8 cm.
Acquisition details unknown.
1989A20.

552
Penannular (ear)ring of circular section tapering
towards pointed overlapping terminals.
Europe, no exact provenance.
Di 2.2 cm.
Purchased Blackmore 1968.
1991A383.

553
Large circular hoop of flattened diamond-shaped
cross-section.
Europe, no provenance.
max. external di. 24 cm.
Purchased Blackmore 1968.
1968A1312.

INDEX OF PROVENANCES

INDEX OF MAJOR TYPES

Concordance of Accession and Catalogue Numbers

Accession	Cat.	Accession	Cat.	Accession	Cat.	Accession	Cat.
1885A1494	87	1953A850.1	2	1964A283	139	1968A1295	206
1885A1499	38	1953A850.2	9	1964A284	98	1968A1296	210
1913A85	137	1953A850.3	1	1965A501	30	1968A1297	216
1930A104.26	110	1953A850.4	3	1965A502	32	1968A1298	215
1930A389	240	1953A850.5	4	1966A30	78	1968A1299	212
1931A68.30	187	1953A850.6	5	1966A32	33	1968A1300	207
1931A68.31	129	1953A850.7	6	1966A33	120	1968A1301	209
1931A68.33	69	1953A850.8	7	1966A34	50	1968A1302	204
1931A68.34	124	1953A850.9	8	1966A35	41	1968A1303	214
1931A68.35	138	1953A850.10	10	1966A36	35	1968A1304	211
1931A68.36	138	1953A851	72	1966A37	128	1968A1305	545
1931A68.37	138	1953A915	535	1966A38	92	1968A1306	541
1933A24	43	1954A19	57	1966A39	90	1968A1307	544
1933A76.2	60	1954A20	84	1966A40	91	1968A1308	546
1935A547.592	105	1954A21	75	1966A41	52	1968A1309	542
1935A547.593	106	1954A22	51	1966A42	117	1968A1310	547
1935A547.594	107	1954A23	369	1966A667.2	95	1968A1311	549
1935A547.595	108	1954A621	42	1966A668.1	13	1968A1312	553
1935A547.596	101	1957A148	132	1966A668.2	12	1968A1313	218
1935A547.597	102	1957A149	131	1966A668.3	11	1968A1314	233
1935A547.598	103	1957A162	111	1966A668.4	14	1968A1315	234
1935A547.599	104	1957A163	112	1966A668.5	19	1968A1316	537
1935A547.600	140	1957A164	109	1966A668.6	15	1968A1317	88
1946A66	47	1957A165	113	1966A668.7	16	1968A1493	222
1948A4.1	38	1957A166	114	1966A668.8	17	1968A1494	221
1948A4.2	43	1957A172	119	1966A668.9	18	1968A1495	242
1948A4.3	47	1957A173	118	1967A1307	54	1968A1499	522
1948A4.4	30	1957A174	121	1967A1308	55	1968A1500	241
1948A4.5	32	1957A175.1	127	1967A1309	56	1968A1501	243
1948A4.6	31	1957A176	59	1967A1310	61	1968A1502	231
1948A4.7	87	1957A177	68	1967A1311	62	1968A1503	230
1948A4.8	66	1957A178	115	1967A1467	86	1968A1504	229
1948A4.9	46	1957A179	134	1968A288	31	1968A1987	370
1948A98	367	1957A180.1	136	1968A1240	195	1969A989	37
1948A99	428	1957A181	135	1968A1241	144	1969A1059	34
1948A100	429	1957A184	185	1968A1242	145	1970A17	100
1948A131	142	1957A185	186	1968A1243	146	1971A17	40
1948A133	548	1957A187	77	1968A1244	150	1972A131	48
1948A134	141	1957A232	116	1968A1245	147	1973A301	45
1948A161	290	1958A4	65	1968A1246	148	1973A302	123
1948A183	80	1958A243.1	22	1968A1247	149	1973A303	122
1948A233.1	525	1958A243.2	23	1968A1248	151	1973A304	126
1948A233.2	524	1958A243.3	24	1968A1249	189	1973A305	125
1949A18	36	1958A243.4	25	1968A1250	190	1973A306	130
1951A605	437	1958A243.5	28	1968A1251	152	1973A307	180
1951A606	436	1958A243.6	29	1968A1252	154	1973A308	176
1951A607	494	1958A243.7	27	1968A1253	156	1973A309	163
1951A608	495	1958A243.8	26	1968A1254	157	1973A310	280
1951A609	374	1962A389	73	1968A1255	153	1973A311	226
1951A611	405	1962A390	85	1968A1256	158	1973A312	227
1951A612	333	1962A391	74	1968A1257	159	1973A316	21
1951A613	358	1962A392	71	1968A1258	160	1973A317	21
1951A614	406	1962A393	89	1968A1259	161	1973A318	21
1951A615	496	1962A394	181	1968A1260	162	1973A319	21
1951A616	432	1962A395	521	1968A1261	165	1973A320	21
1951A617	334	1962A396	515	1968A1262	194	1973A321	21
1951A618	403	1962A397	520	1968A1263	192	1973A322	21
1951A619	486	1962A398	44	1968A1264	193	1973A323	21
1951A620	487	1962A399	70	1968A1264.1	202	1973A324	21
1951A621	488	1962A401	533	1968A1265	203	1973A325	21
1951A622	479	1962A402	550	1968A1266	197	1973A326.1	20
1951A623	480	1962A403	536	1968A1267	196	1973A326.2	21
1951A624	481	1962A404	538	1968A1268	143	1973A326.3	21
1951A625	482	1962A405	543	1968A1269	166	1973A326.4	21
1951A627	483	1962A406	523	1968A1270	168	1973A1247	99
1951A721	510	1962A407	540	1968A1271	182	1973A1341	81
1951A722	266	1962A408	526	1968A1272	178	1973A1350	228
1951A723	301	1963A174	223	1968A1273	179	1973A1351	83
1951A724	302	1963A901	96	1968A1274	177	1973A1352	82
1951A725	257	1963A902	539	1968A1292	208	1973A1353	232
1951A726	258	1964A2	527	1968A1293	213	1973A1354	169
1953A688	93	1964A113	97	1968A1294	205	1973A1355	53

Concordance of Accession and Catalogue Numbers

1975A112	167	1983A278	402	1983A350	509	1983A532	173
1975A113	175	1983A279	398	1983A351	328	1983A533	184
1975A114	174	1983A280	401	1983A352	329	1983A534	217
1982A2400	528	1983A281	404	1983A353	327	1983A809	246
1982A3079	67	1983A282	400	1983A354	330	1983A810	245
1983A109	79	1983A283	399	1983A355	325	1983A811	244
1983A111	63	1983A284	413	1983A356	324	1983A812	155
1983A112	58	1983A285	411	1983A357	247	1983A813	514
1983A113	49	1983A286	408	1983A358	248	1983A814	516
1983A215	317	1983A287	407	1983A359	249	1983A815	164
1983A216	315	1983A288	357	1983A360	250	1983A816	517
1983A217	311	1983A289	359	1983A361	256	1983A817	519
1983A218	313	1983A290	360	1983A362	267	1983A818	188
1983A219	307	1983A291	335	1983A363	268	1983A819	531
1983A220	294	1983A292	361	1983A364	269	1983A820	530
1983A221	298	1983A293	353	1983A399	439	1983A821	529
1983A222	291	1983A294	336	1983A400	438	1983A822	219
1983A223	316	1983A295	337	1983A401	440	1983A823	532
1983A224	292	1983A296	338	1983A402	198	1983A824	220
1983A225	295	1983A297	339	1983A403	199	1983A846	235
1983A226	297	1983A298	340	1983A404	462	1983A847	236
1983A227	310	1983A299	425	1983A405	463	1983A1031	373
1983A228	306	1983A300	341	1983A406	454	1983A1032	368
1983A229	304	1983A301	342	1983A407	461	1983A1033	423
1983A230	303	1983A302	343	1983A408	465	1983A1034	349
1983A231	308	1983A303	362	1983A409	464	1983A1035	350
1983A232	309	1983A304	363	1983A410	458	1983A1036	351
1983A233	305	1983A305	364	1983A411	460	1983A1037	414
1983A234	312	1983A306	355	1983A412	457	1983A1038	415
1983A235	299	1983A307	427	1983A413	455	1983A1039	416
1983A236	296	1983A308	344	1983A414	456	1983A1040	417
1983A237	318	1983A309	345	1983A415	459	1983A1041	418
1983A238	320	1983A310	352	1983A416	469	1983A1042	424
1983A239	321	1983A311	365	1983A417	447	1983A1043	500
1983A240	319	1983A312	346	1983A418	449	1983A1044	393
1983A241	270	1983A313	331	1983A419	448	1983A1045	394
1983A242	238	1983A314	356	1983A420	508	1983A1046	395
1983A243	285	1983A315	354	1983A421	451	1983A1047	396
1983A244	284	1983A316	347	1983A422	450	1983A1048	397
1983A245	287	1983A317	420	1983A423	264	1983A1049	366
1983A246	286	1983A318	332	1983A424	265	1983A1050	253
1983A247	237	1983A319	348	1983A425	201	1983A1051	260
1983A248	288	1983A320	422	1983A426	484	1983A1052	263
1983A249	289	1983A321	421	1983A427	485	1983A1053	498
1983A250	251	1983A322	426	1983A428	475	1983A1054	452
1983A251	252	1983A323	371	1983A429	476	1983A1055	200
1983A252	254	1983A324	372	1983A430	477	1983A1056	453
1983A253	430	1983A325	283	1983A431	478	1983A1057	470
1983A254	375	1983A326	272	1983A432	492	1983A1058	497
1983A255	376	1983A327	278	1983A433	491	1983A1059	293
1983A256	377	1983A328	279	1983A434	493	1983A1060	300
1983A257	378	1983A329	191	1983A435	502	1983A1061	314
1983A258	379	1983A330	273	1983A436	513	1983A1062	322
1983A259	380	1983A331	274	1983A437	441	1985A32	39
1983A260	431	1983A332	275	1983A438	442	1985A33	64
1983A261	381	1983A333	276	1983A439	443	1987A218	76
1983A262	382	1983A334	277	1983A440	444	1987A346	170
1983A263	383	1983A335	271	1983A441	445	1987A347	171
1983A264	384	1983A336	281	1983A442	446	1987A348	518
1983A265	385	1983A337	282	1983A443	473	1987A349	183
1983A266	386	1983A338	255	1983A444	472	1989A14	225
1983A267	387	1983A339	259	1983A445	503	1989A15	224
1983A268	388	1983A340	326	1983A446	504	1989A16	239
1983A269	389	1983A341	507	1983A447	468	1989A18	133
1983A270	390	1983A342	506	1983A448	466	1989A19	534
1983A271	391	1983A343	501	1983A449	512	1989A20	551
1983A272	392	1983A344	505	1983A450	434	1989A21	490
1983A273	409	1983A345	261	1983A451	471	1989A22	489
1983A274	419	1983A346	262	1983A452	467	1991A381	94
1983A275	410	1983A347	435	1983A453	323	1991A383	552
1983A276	412	1983A348	499	1983A454	511		
1983A277	433	1983A349	474	1983A531	172		

BIBLIOGRAPHY

Abbreviations used

AJA   American Journal of Archaeology
BAR   British Archaeological Reports
BNJ   The British Numismatic Journal
PBF   Prähistorische Bronzefunde
PPS   Proceedings of the Prehistoric Society
SAC   Surrey Archaeological Collections
TBAS   Transactions of the Birmingham [and Warwickshire] Archaeological Society
TSSAHS Transactions of the South Staffordshire Archaeological and Historical Society
TWAS   Transactions of the Worcestershire Archaeological Society
WMA   West Midlands Archaeology

Alexander, J., 1965. 'The Spectacle Fibulae of Southern Europe', *AJA* 69, 7–23.
Audouze, F. and Courtois, J.-C., 1970. *Les Epingles du Sud-Est de la France*, PBF XIII/I (München).
Bietti-Sestieri, A.M., 1973. 'The Metal Industry of Continental Italy, 13th to the 11th century BC, and its connections with the Aegean', *PPS* 39, 383–424.
Bishop, M.W., 1977. 'Bronze Spearhead from Leamington Spa', *TBAS* 88, 127.
Briard, J., 1965. *Les Depots Bretons et L'Age du Bronze Atlantique*. (Rennes).
Burgess, C.B. and Gerloff, S., 1981. *The Dirks and Rapiers of Great Britain and Ireland*, PBF IV/7 (München).
Caunce, L.I., 1982. *The Swiss Lake Material in the Merseyside County Museums, Studied in the Context of its Historical, Ecological and Cultural Background*. Unpublished BA Dissertation. Liverpool.
Chardenoux, M.-B. and Courtois, J.-C. 1979. *Les haches dans la France Méridionale*, PBF IX/II (München).
Chatwin, P.B., 1922. 'The Staunton Collection', *TBAS* XLVIII, 171–176.
Clarke, D.L., 1970. *Beaker Pottery of Great Britain and Ireland*. (Cambridge).
Coles, J., 1963. 'The Hilton (Dorset) Gold Ornaments', *Antiquity* 37, 132–134.
Collyer, H.C., 1908. 'Bronze Implements Found at Carshalton and Croydon', *SAC* XXI, 208.
Colquhoun, I. and Burgess, C.B., 1988. *The Swords of Britain*, PBF IV/5 (München).
Davey, P.J., 1973. 'Bronze Age Metalwork from Lincolnshire', *Archaeologia* 104, 51–127.
Eogan, G., 1965. *Catalogue of Irish Bronze Swords* (Dublin).
Fox, C., 1958. *Pattern and Purpose – A Survey of Early Celtic Art in Britain*. (Cardiff).
Gimbutas, M., 1965. *Bronze Age Cultures in Central and Eastern Europe*. (The Hague).
Gunstone, A.J.H., 1965. 'Chance Finds Reported to the City of Birmingham Museum', *TBAS* 82 (1965), 93–96.
Gunstone, A.J.H., 1971. *Sylloge of Coins of the British Isles 17: Ancient British Anglo-Saxon and Norman Coins in Midlands Museums*. (London).
Gunstone, A.J.H., 1972. 'Some Prehistoric Implements from South Staffordshire Reported to the Birmingham City Museum', *TSSAHS* 13, 46–50.
Harbison, P., 1969. *The Axes of the Early Bronze Age in Ireland*, PBF IX/I (München).
Hattat, R., 1987. *Brooches of Antiquity – A third selection of brooches from the author's collection*. (Oxford).
Hull, M.R. and Hawkes, C.F.C., 1987. *Corpus of Ancient Brooches in Britain – Pre-Roman Bow Brooches*. BAR British Series 168. (Oxford).
Humphreys, H.F., 1944. 'A Bronze Age Palstave found near Kenilworth', *TBAS* 65, 141–142.
Keller, F., 1878. *The Lake Dwellings of Switzerland and Other Parts of Europe*. (London).
Malam, J.P., 1981. 'Find of Late Bronze Age Socketed Axe and Wooden Shaft fragment', *WMA* 24, 131–134.
Mitchell, L., 1923. 'Implement found at Curdworth', *TBAS* 49, 76.
Moore, W.R.G., 1977. 'Archaeology in Northamptonshire 1976, Oundle', *Northamptonshire Archaeology* 12, 209.
Munro, R., 1890. *The Lake Dwellings of Europe being the Rhind Lectures in Archaeology for 1888*. (London).
Painter, K.S., 1970. 'An Iron Age Gold Alloy Torc from Glascote, Tamworth, Staffordshire', *TSSAHS* XI, 1–6.
Peltenburg, E.J., 1981. *Cypriot Antiquities in Birmingham Museum and Art Gallery*. (Birmingham).
Phillips, W.E., 1967. 'Bronze Age Metal Objects in Surrey', *SAC* LXIV, 1–34.
Phillips, W.E., 1968. 'A Note on the Carshalton Hoard', *SAC* LXV, 130–133.
Piggot, C.M., 1946. 'The Late Bronze Age Razors of the British Isles', *PPS* 12, 121–141
Roberts, R., 1882. 'A Description of some Ancient Gold Ornaments found in Dorsetshire', *Proceedings of the Dorset Natural History and Antiquarian Field Club* IV, 158–159.
Rowlands, M.J., 1976. *The Organization of Middle Bronze Age Metalworking*, BAR British Series 31. (Oxford).

Bibliography

Sandars, N.K., 1950. 'Daggers as type fossils in the French Early Bronze Age', *University of London Institute of Archaeology 6th Annual Report*, 44–59.

Sandars, N.K., 1957. *Bronze Age Cultures in France*. (Cambridge).

Simpson, W.G., 1976. 'A Barrow Cemetery of the Second Millennium BC at Tallington, Lincolnshire', *PPS* 42, 215–239.

Smith, C.N.S., 1957. 'A Catalogue of the Prehistoric Finds from Worcestershire', *TWAS* N.S. 34, 1–27.

Sulimirski, T., 1964. 'Barrow Grave 6 at Komaròw', *University of London Institute of Archaeology Bulletin* 4, 171–188.

Symons, D.J., 1988. 'Coin Register', *BNJ* 58, 144, 145–146, 147.

Taylor, J.J., 1980. *Bronze Age Goldwork of the British Isles*. (Cambridge).

Thomas, N., 1970. 'A Palstave from King's Heath, Birmingham', *TBAS* 84, 180.

Trump, B.A.V., 1962. 'The Origin and Development of British Middle Bronze Age Rapiers', *PPS* 28, 80–102.

Vine, P.M., 1982. *The Neolithic and Bronze Age Cultures of the Middle and Upper Trent Basin*. BAR British Series 105. (Oxford).

Watson, P.J., 1984. 'Some New Middle and Late Bronze Age Axes from South Staffordshire and West Midlands', *TBAS* 93, 1–7.

Watson, P.J., 1988a. 'An Early British Sword from Solihull', *TBAS* 95, 103–107.

Watson, P.J., 1988b. 'Two Recent Bronze Age Finds from Worcestershire', *TWAS* 3rd Series, 11, 23–26.

Windle, B.C.A., 1904. *Remains of the Prehistoric Age in England*. (London).

ILLUSTRATIONS

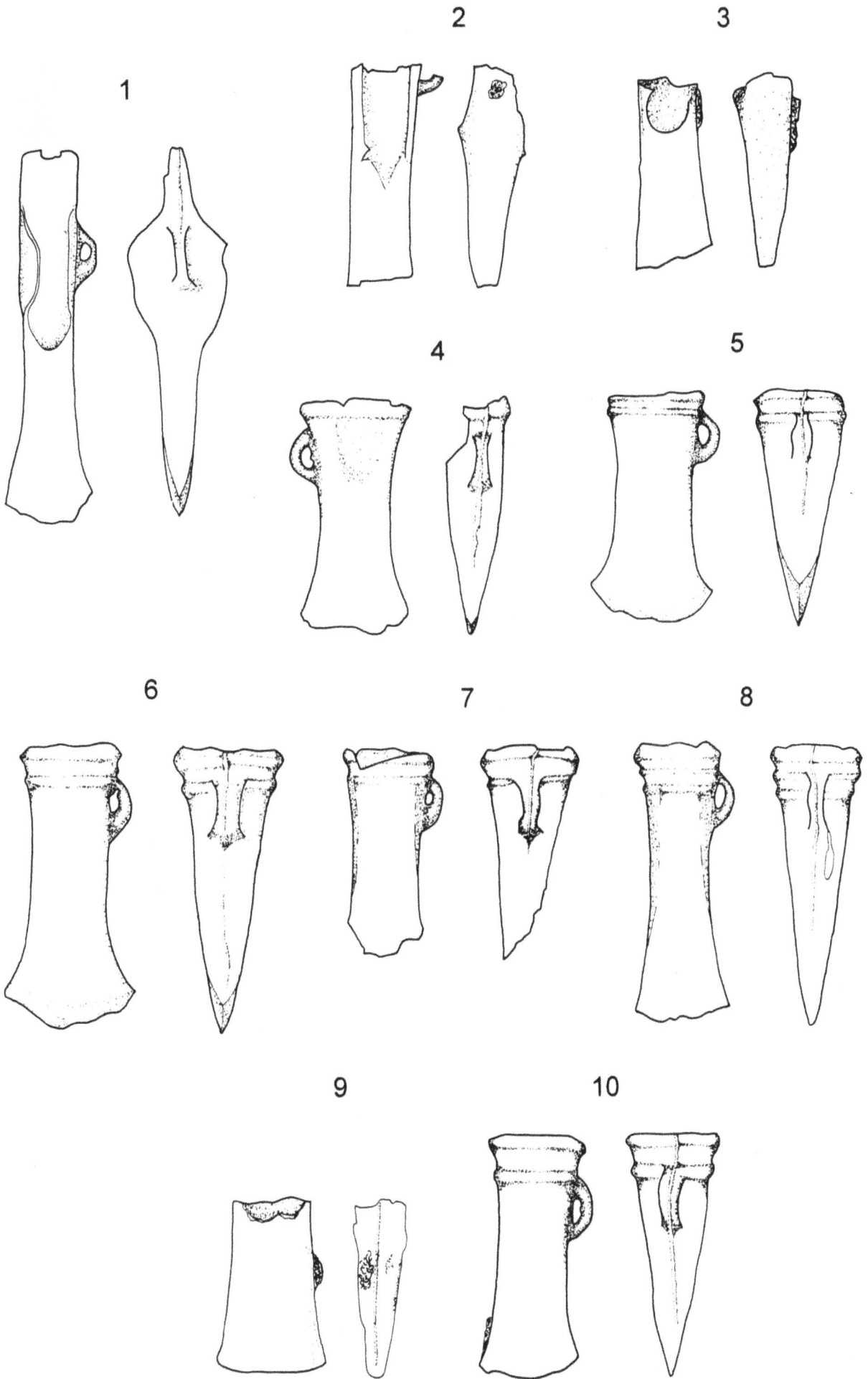

11

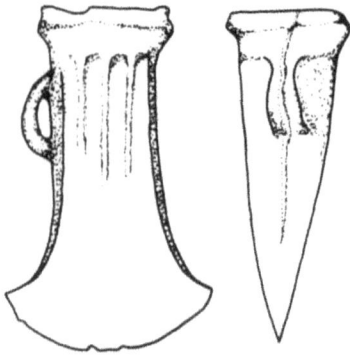

12

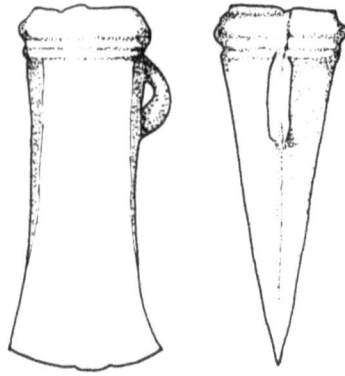

13

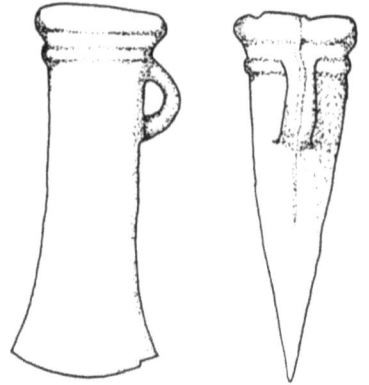

14

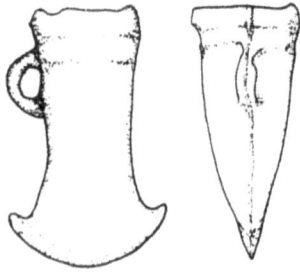

15

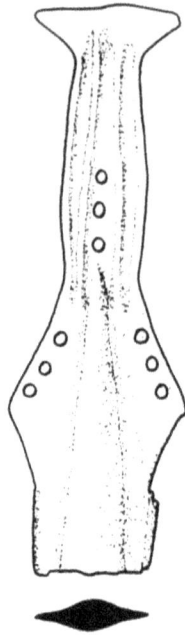

16

17

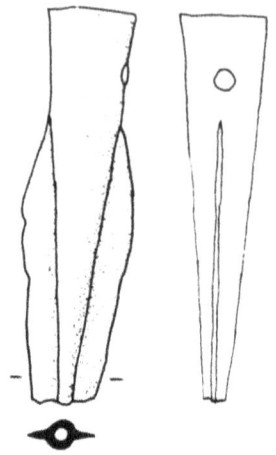

18

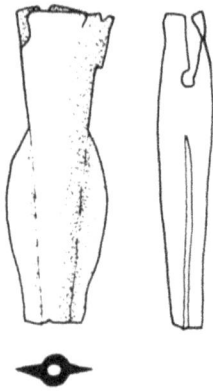

19

20

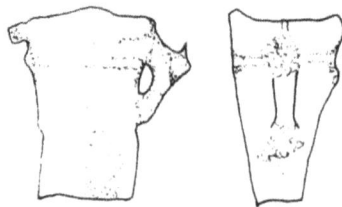

21

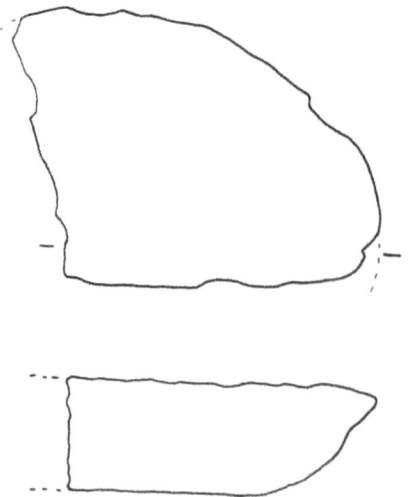

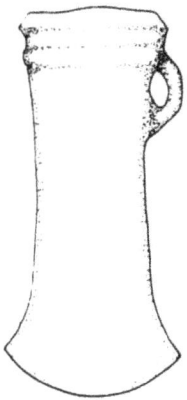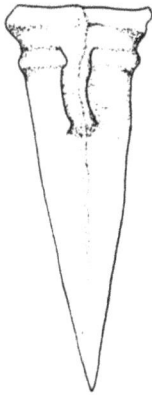
22

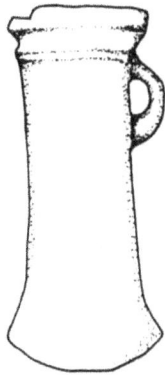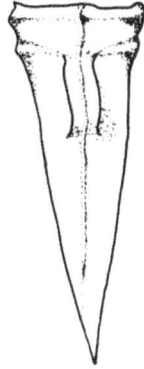
23

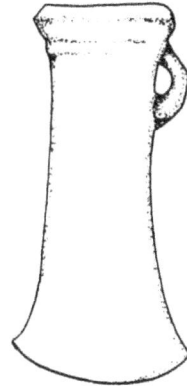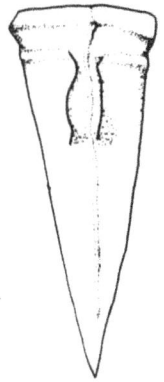
24

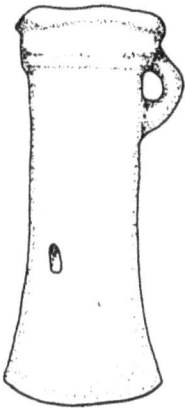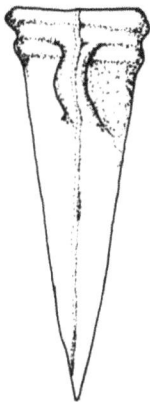
25

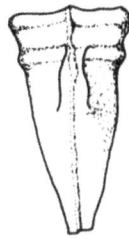
26

27

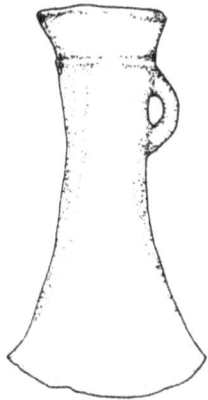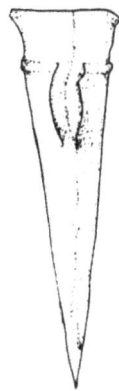
28

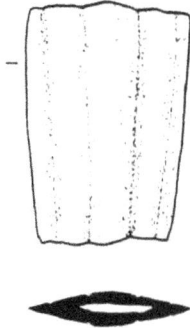
29

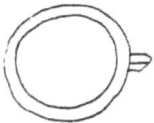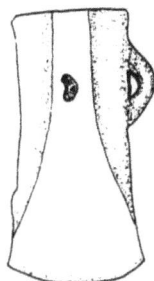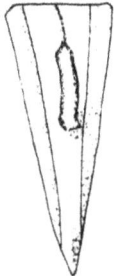
30

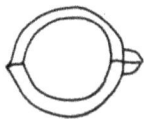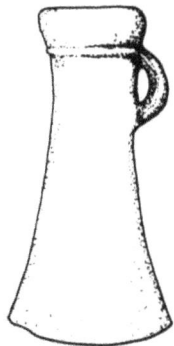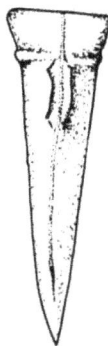
31

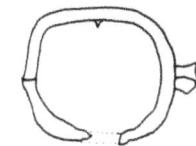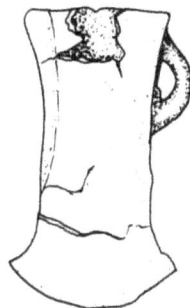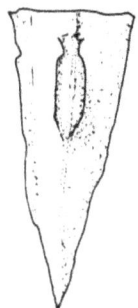
32

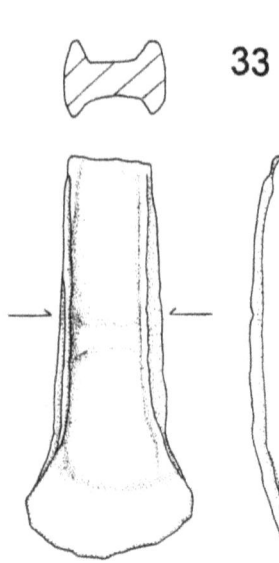

33

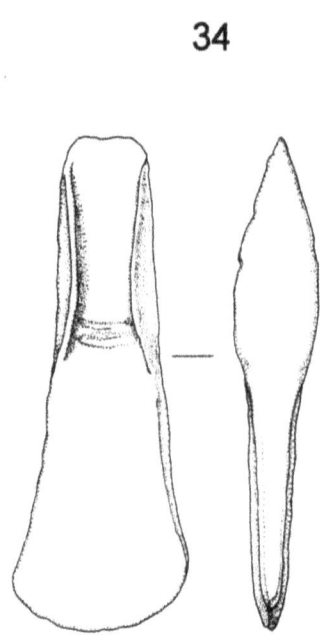

34

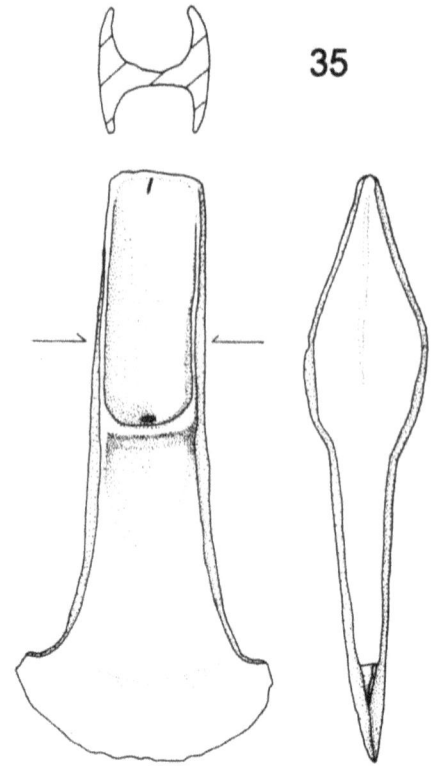

35

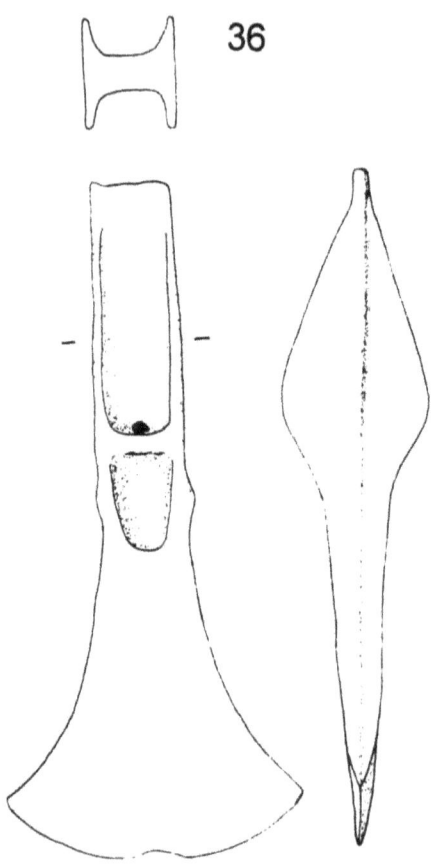

36

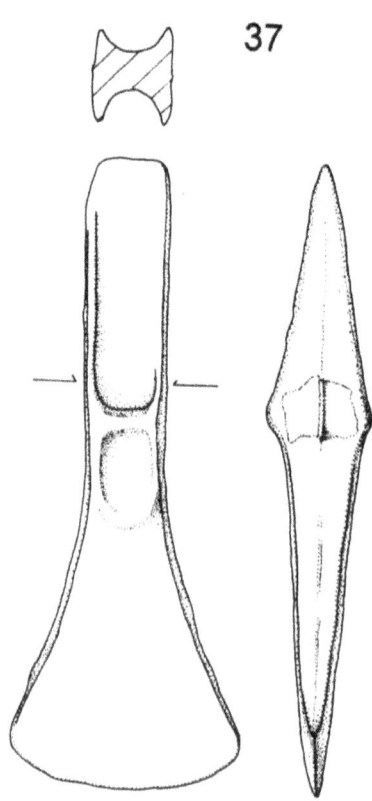

37

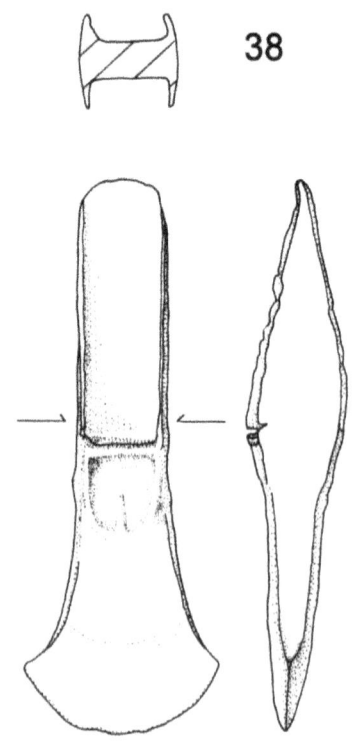

38

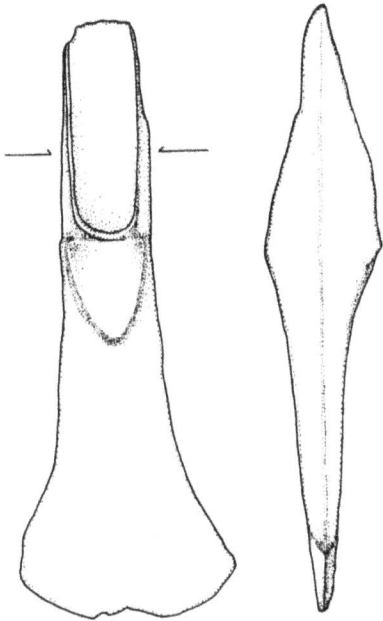

39

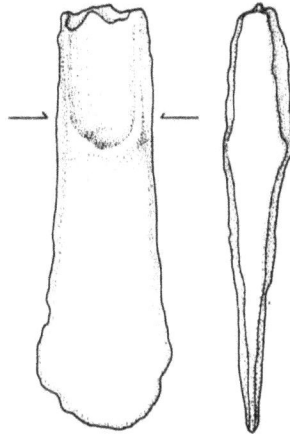

40

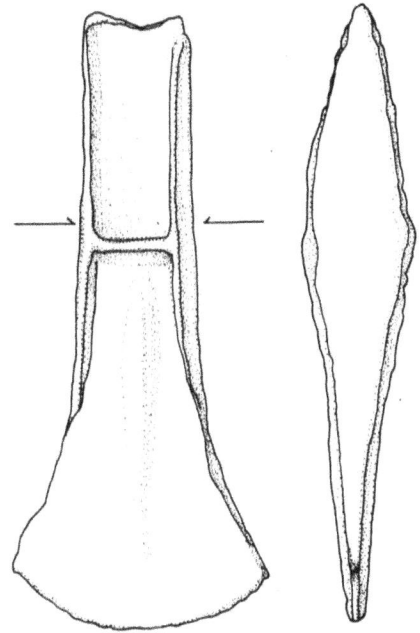

41

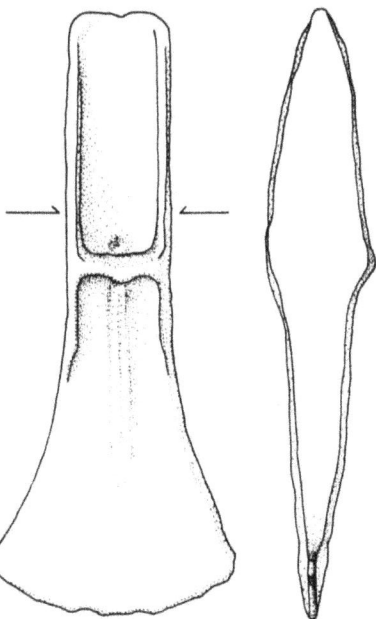

42

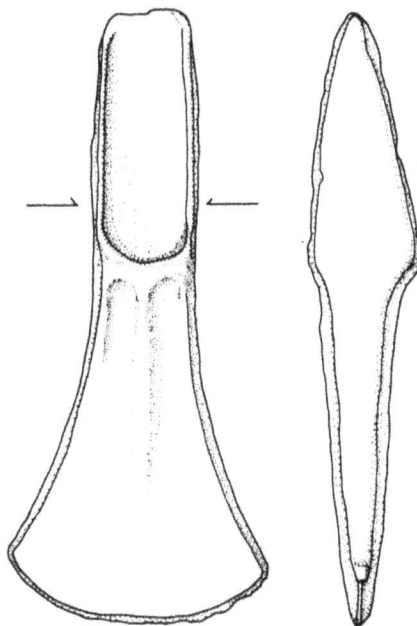

43

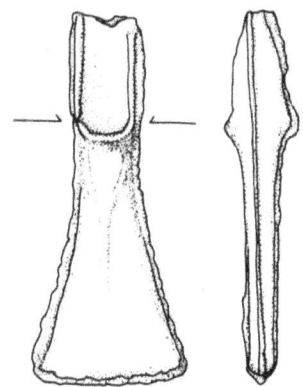

44

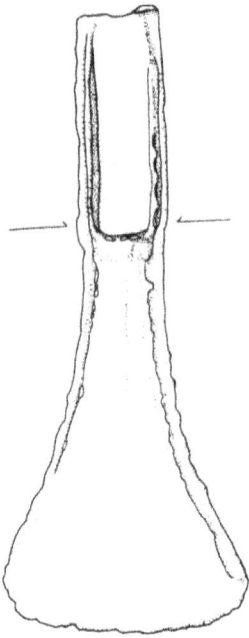
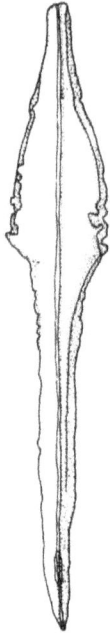

45

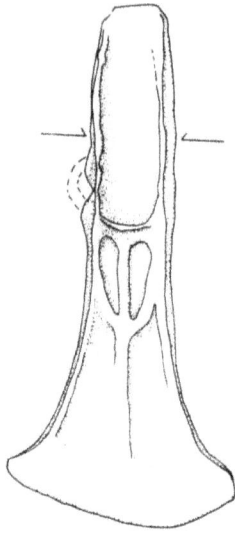
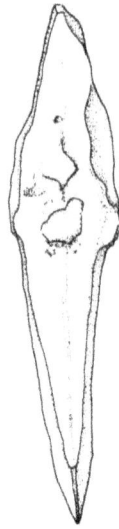

46

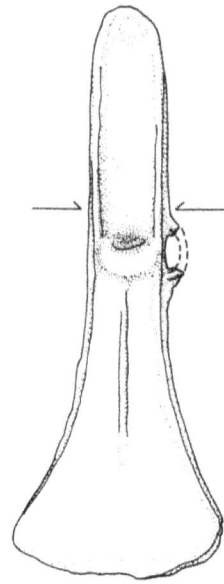
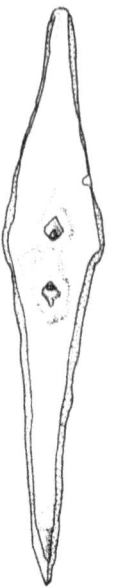

47

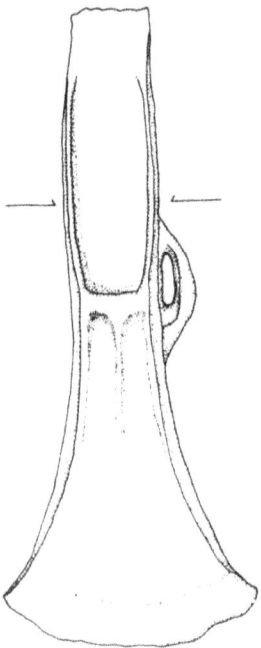

48

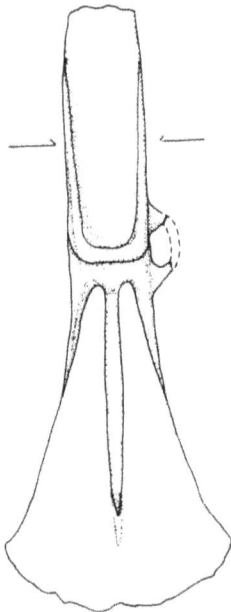
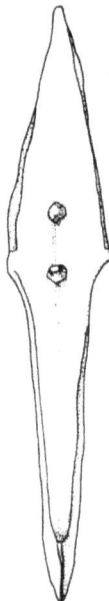

49

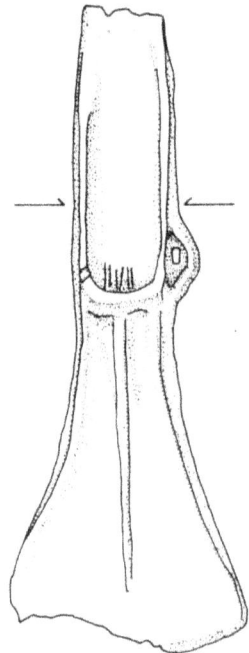
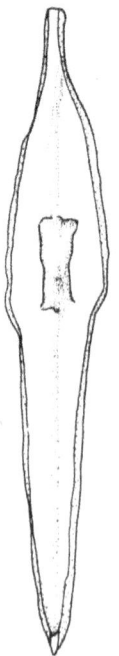

50

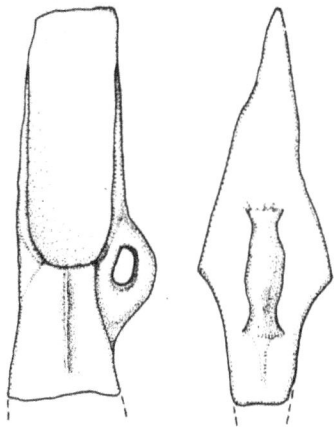

51

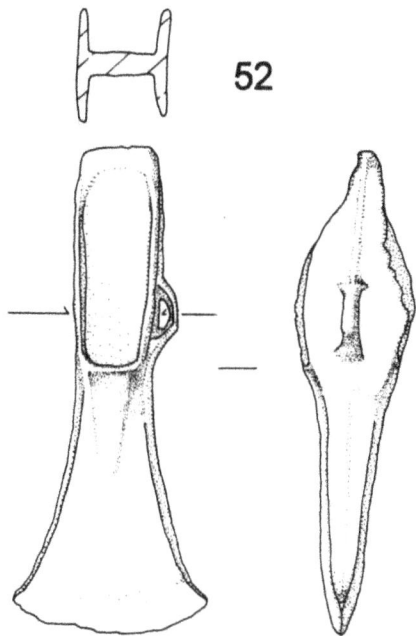

52

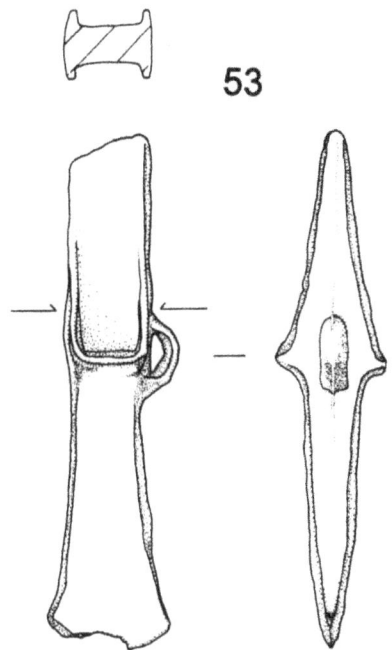

53

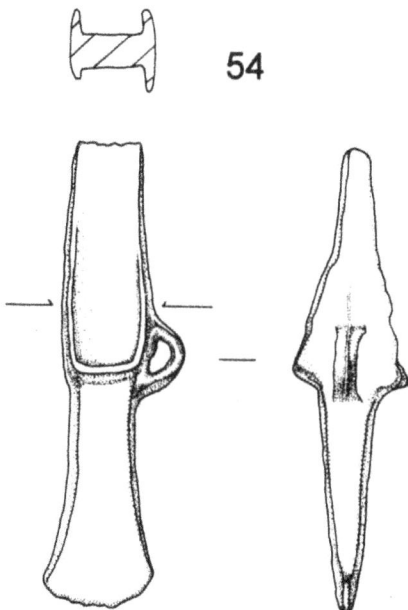

54

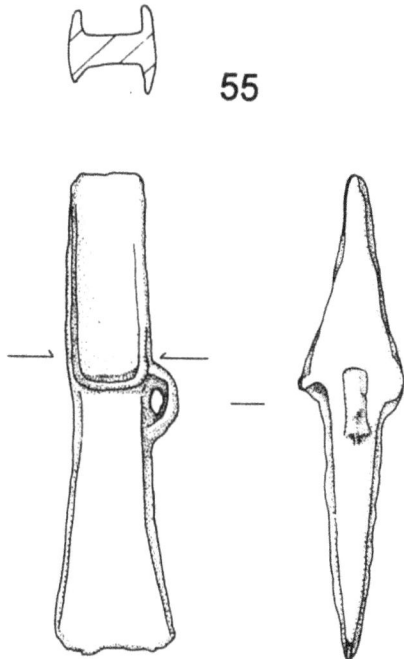

55

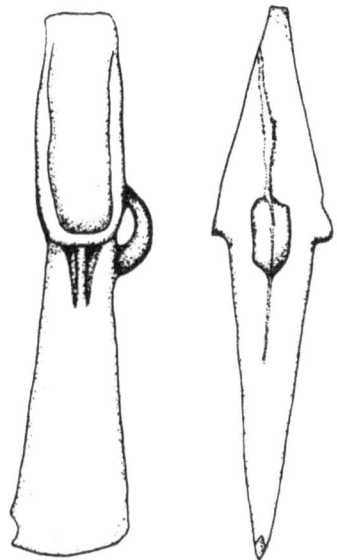

56

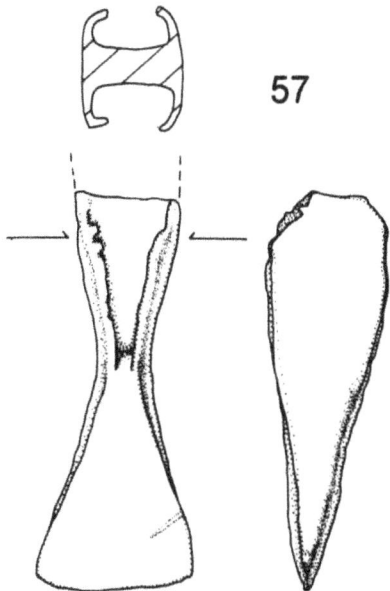

57

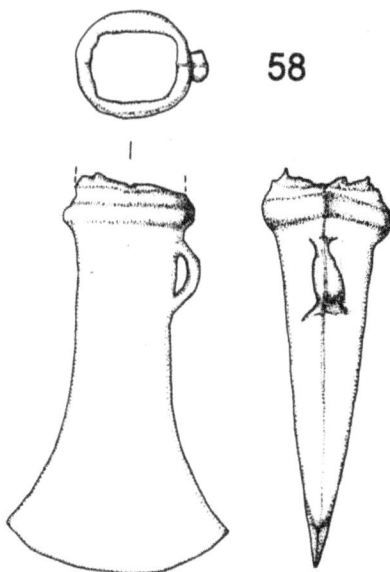

58

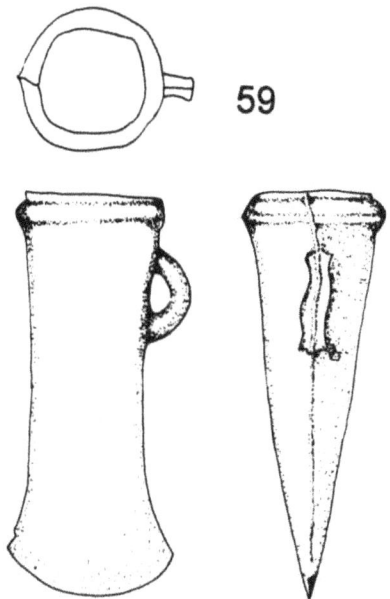

59

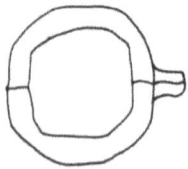
60

61

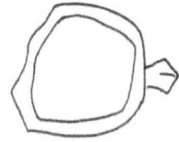
62

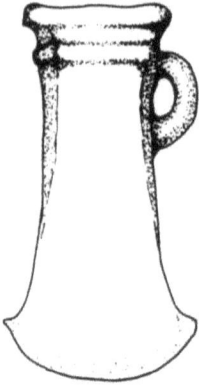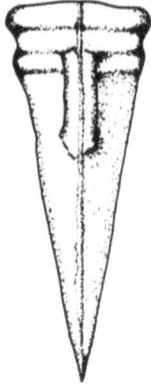
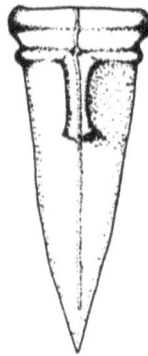
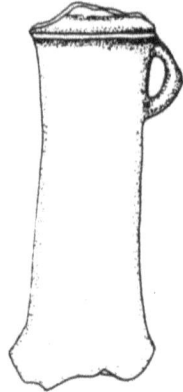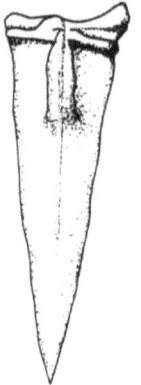

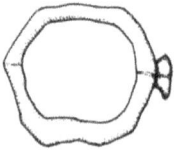
63

64

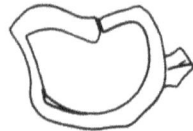
65

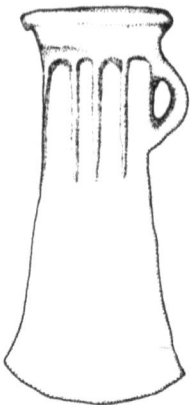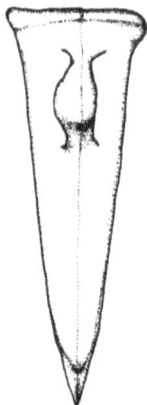

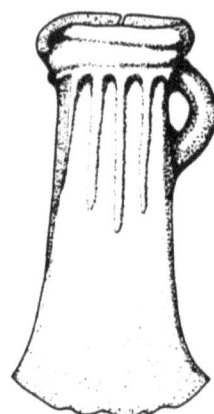

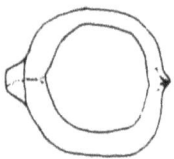
66

67

68

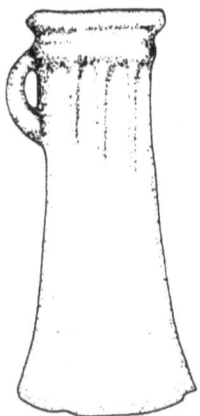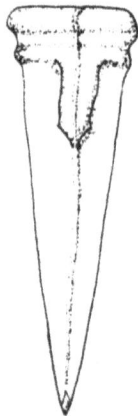
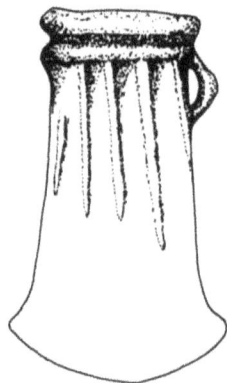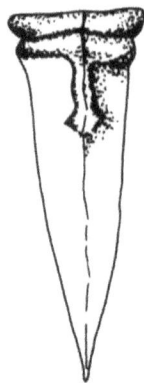
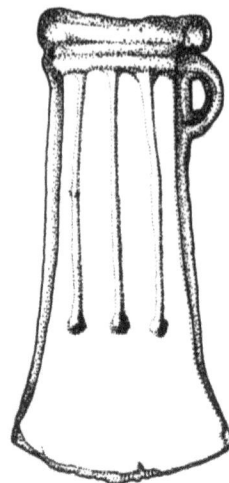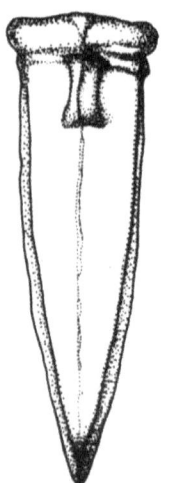

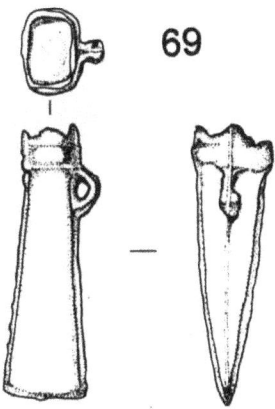

69

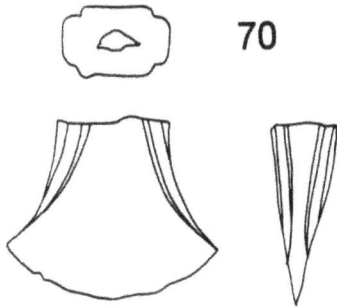

70

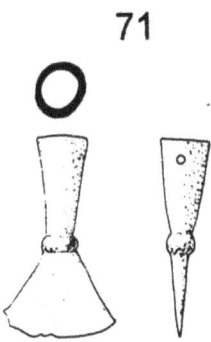

71

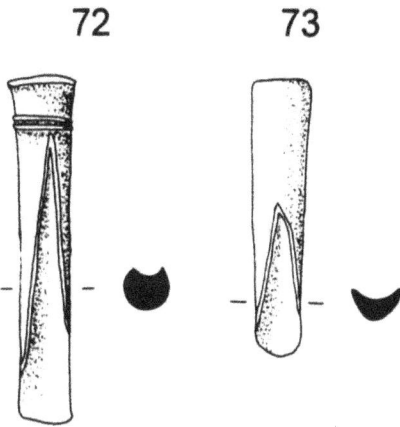

72

73

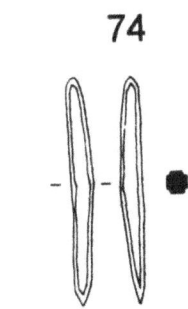

74

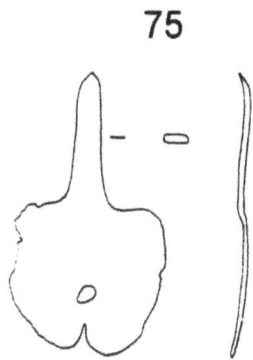

75

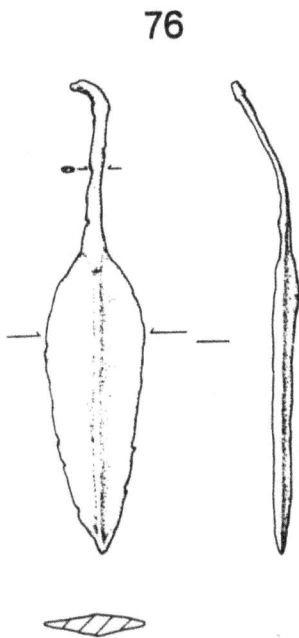

76

77

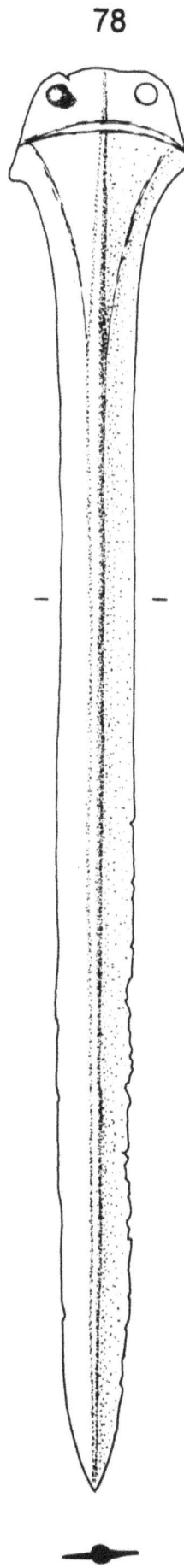

78

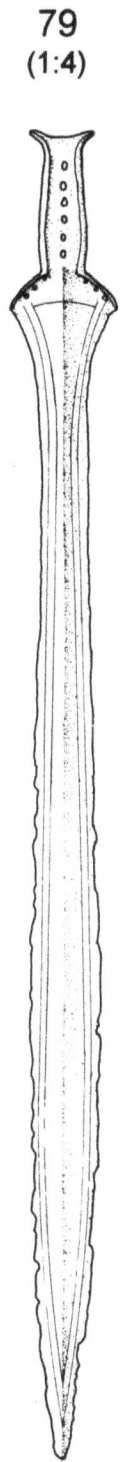

79
(1:4)

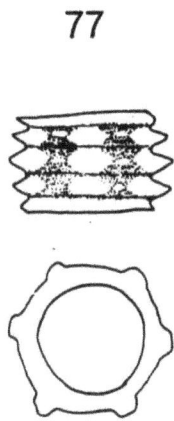

80

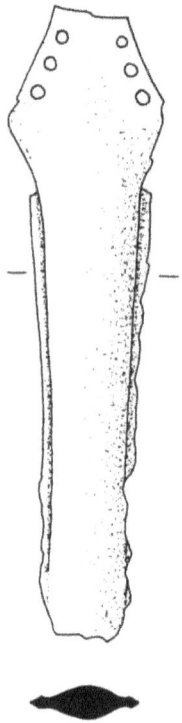

81

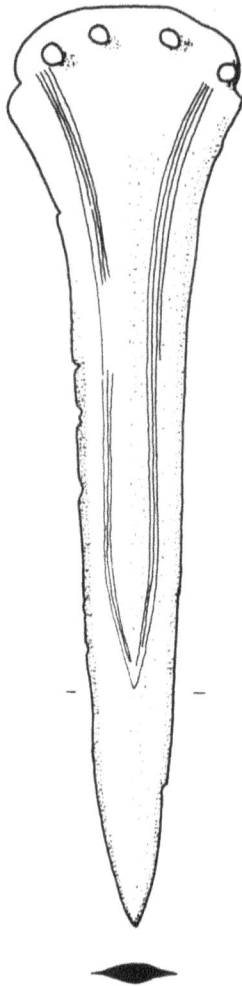

82

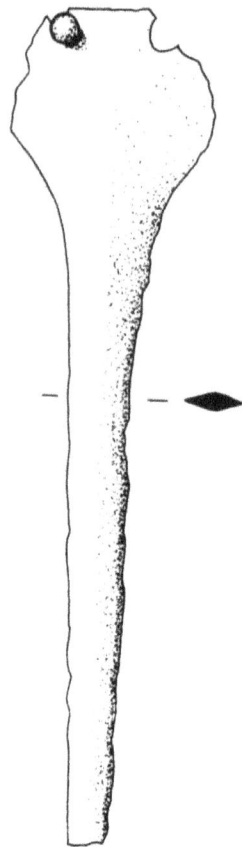

83

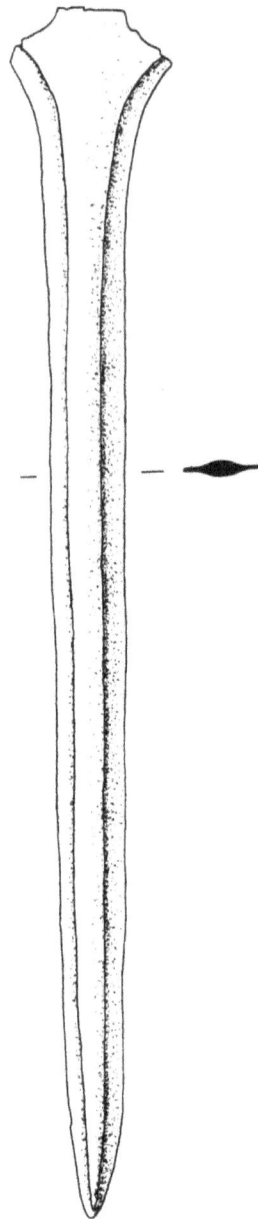

84

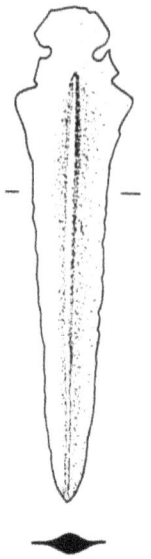

85

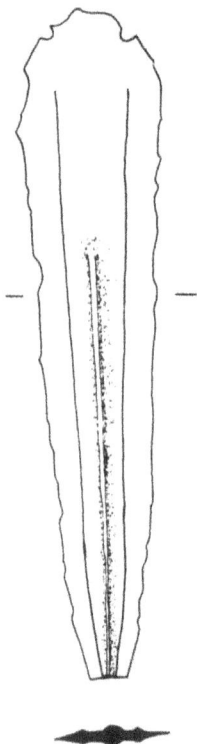

86

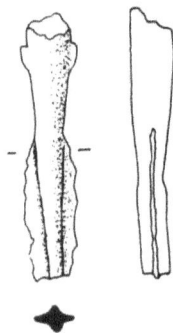

87

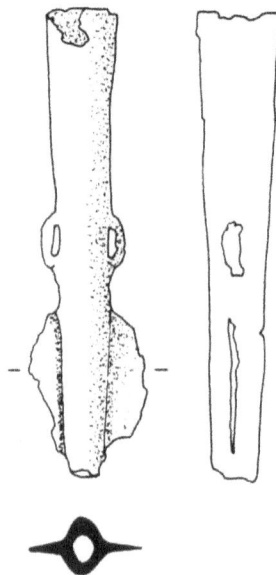

88

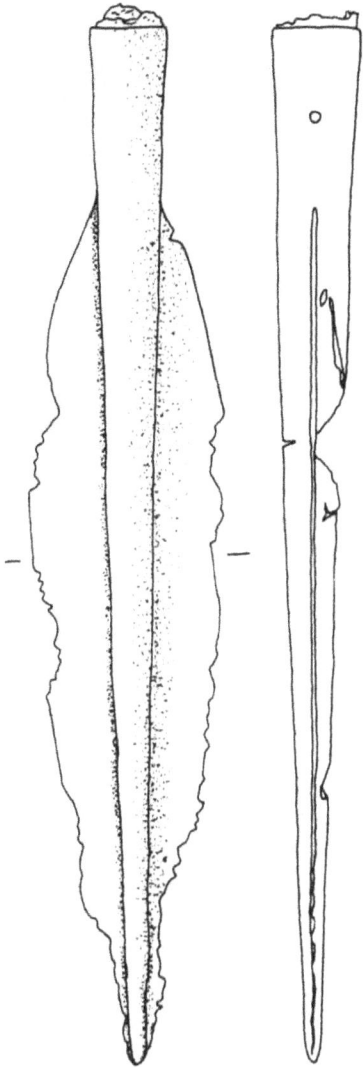

89

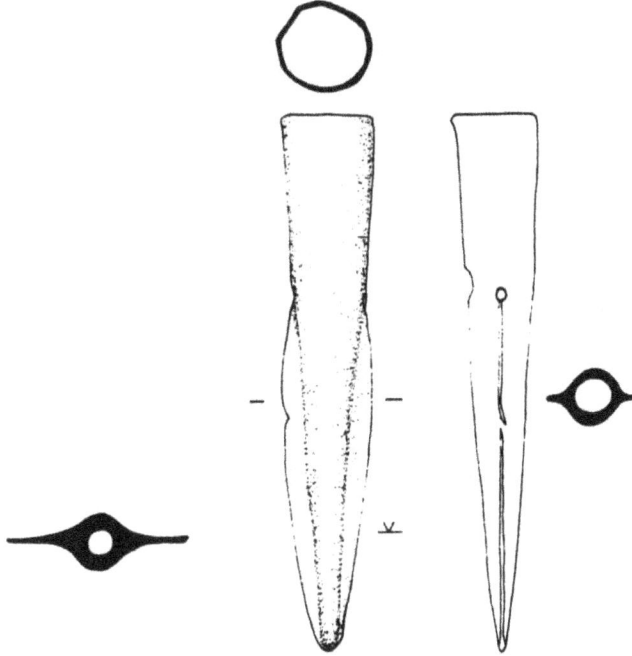

90

91

92

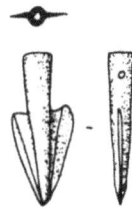

93

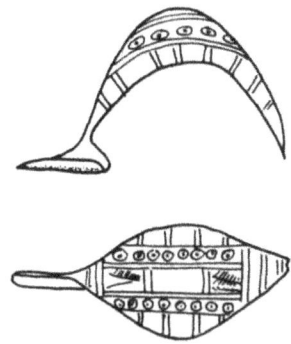

94

95

96

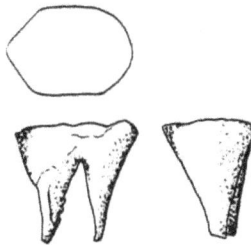

97 - 100
See plates I - III

99

101

102

103

104

105

106

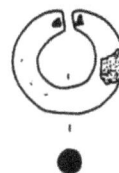

107

108

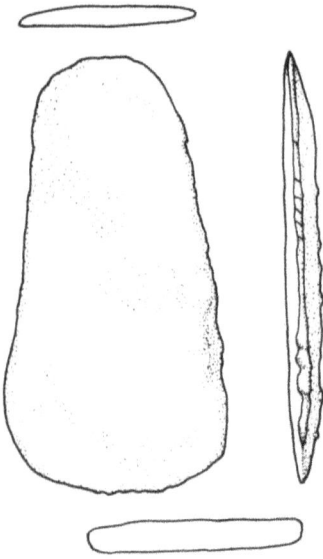

109

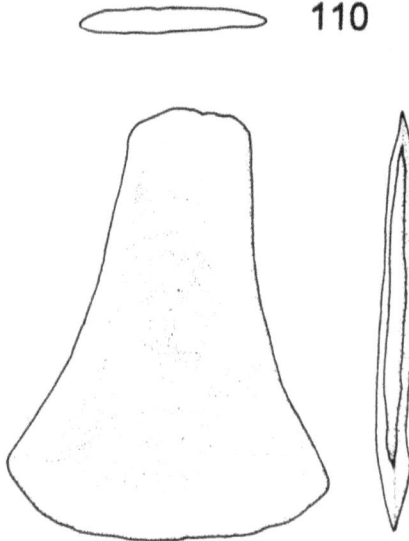

110

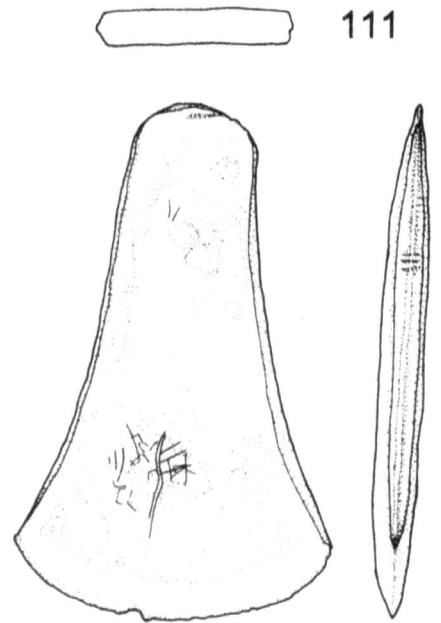

111

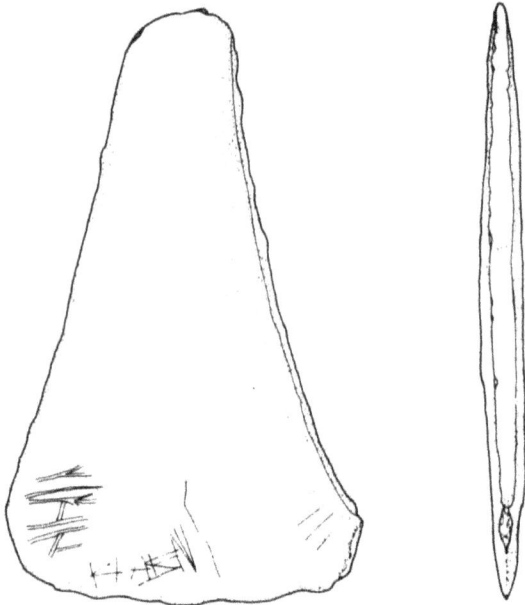

112

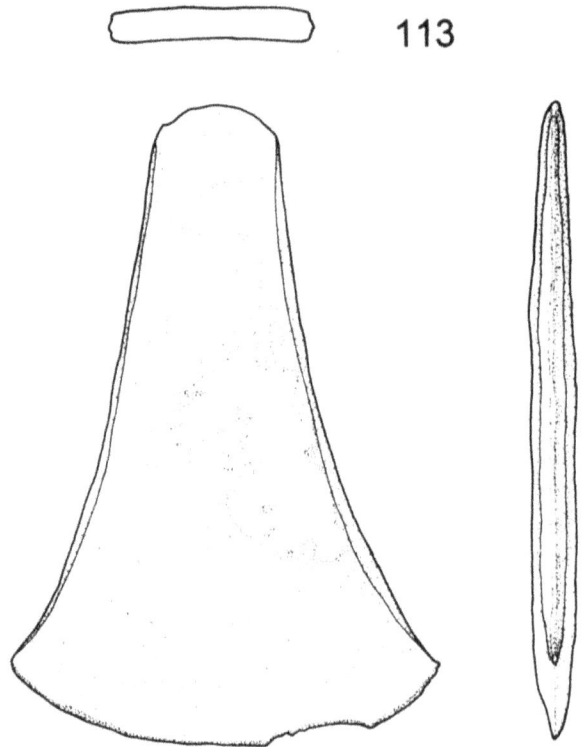

113

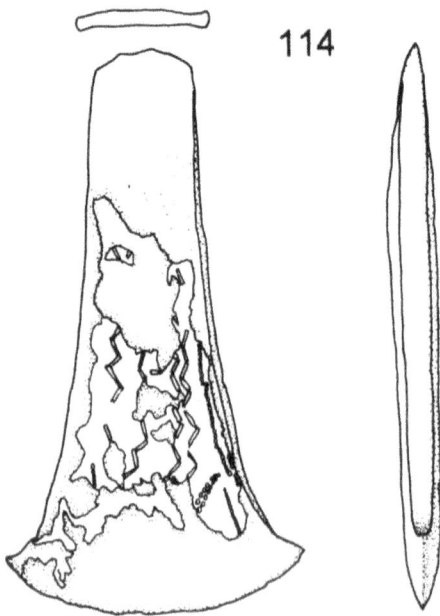

114

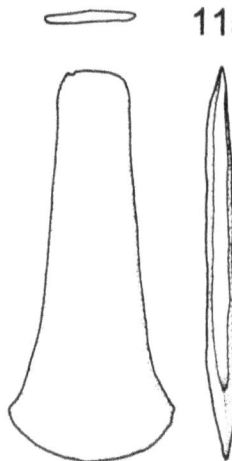

115

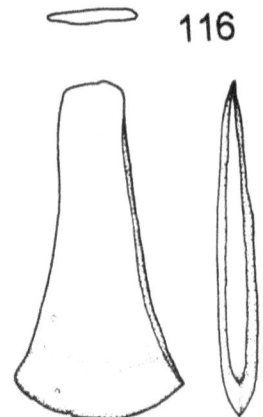

116

117

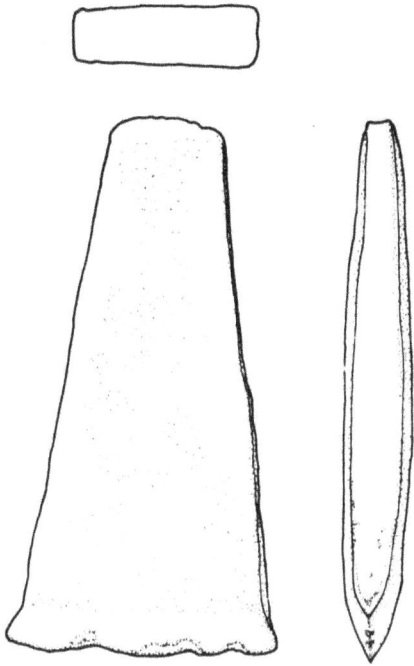

118

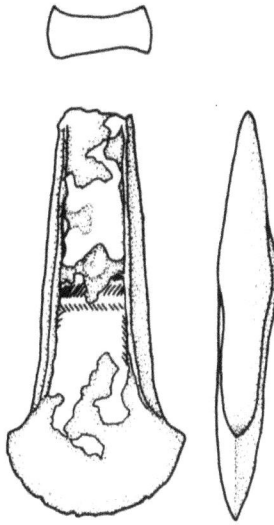

119

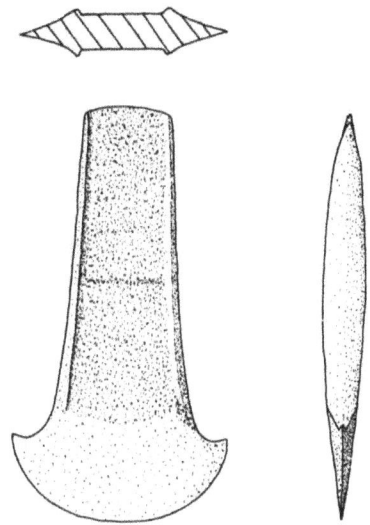

120

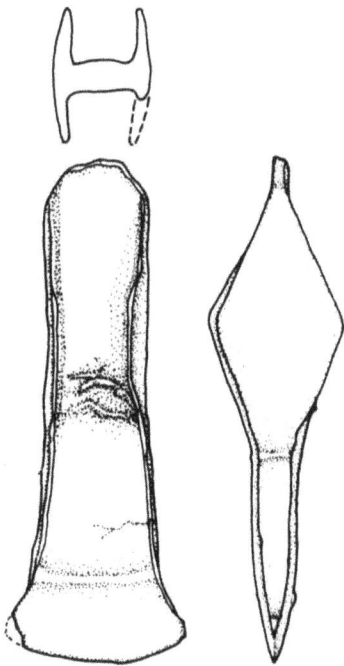

121

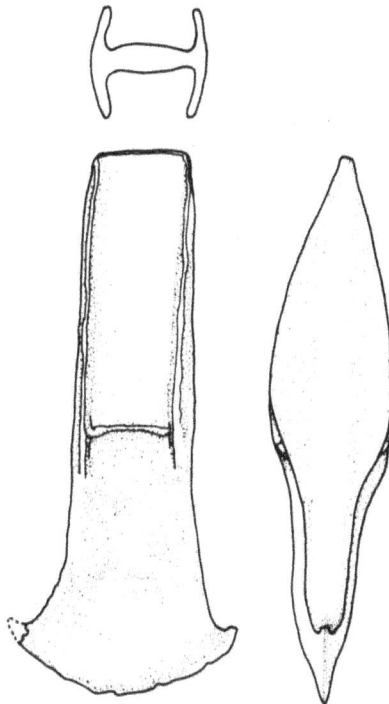

122

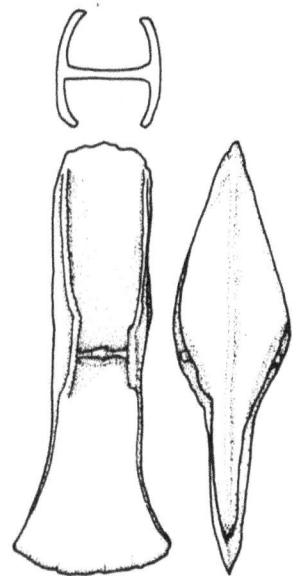

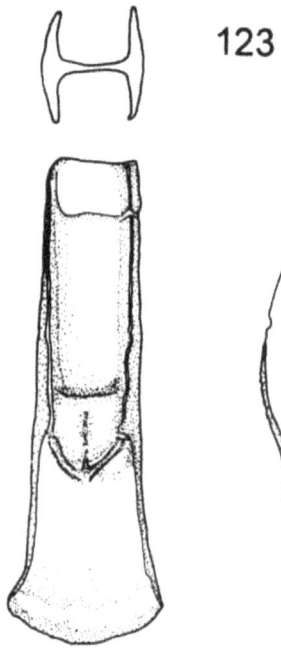

123

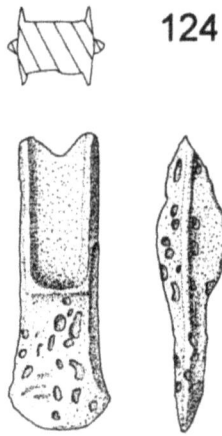

124

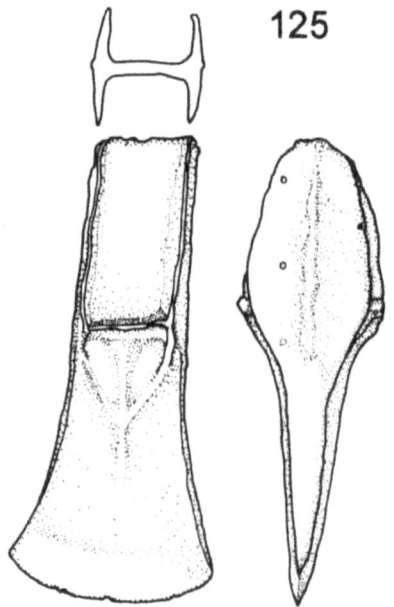

125

128

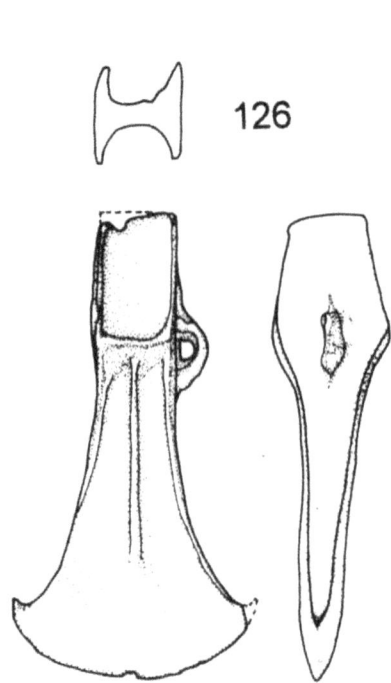

126

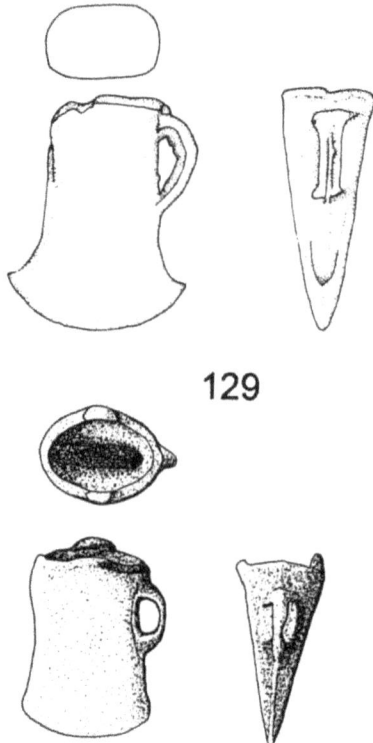

129

131

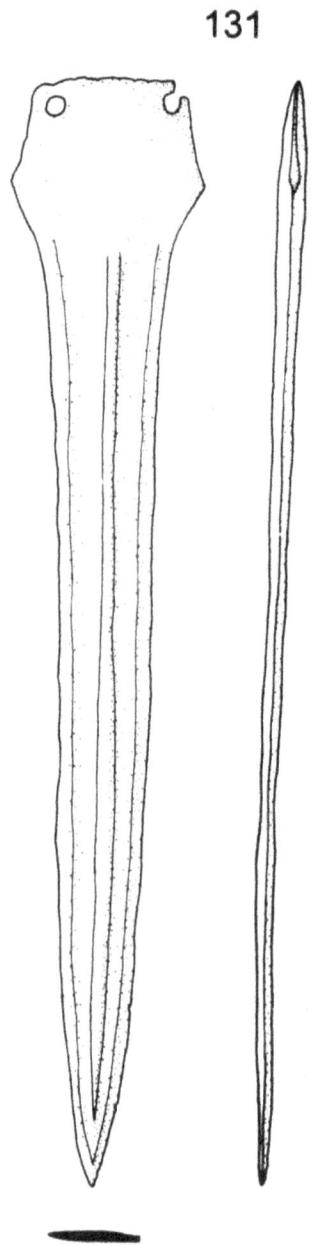

127

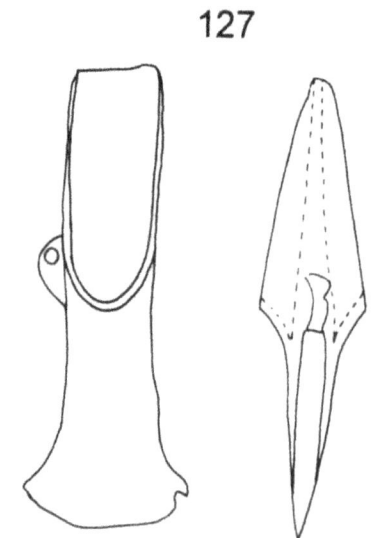

130

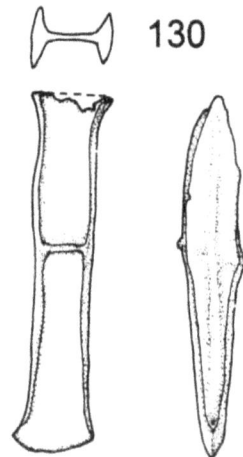

132

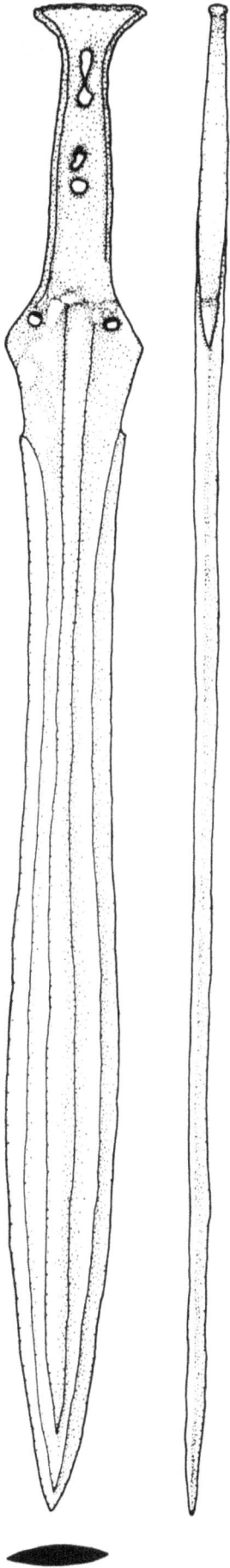

133

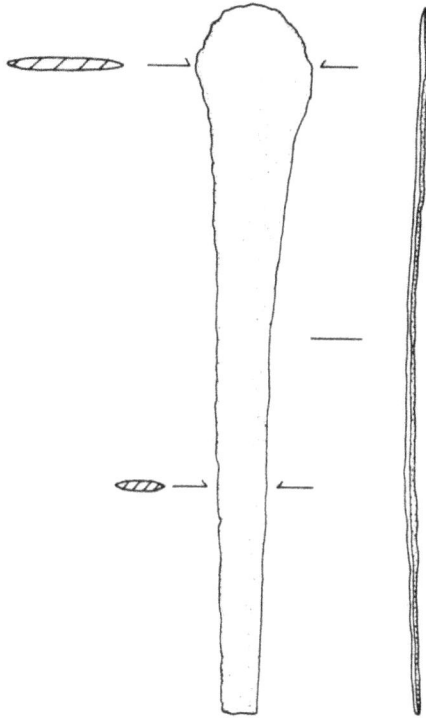

134

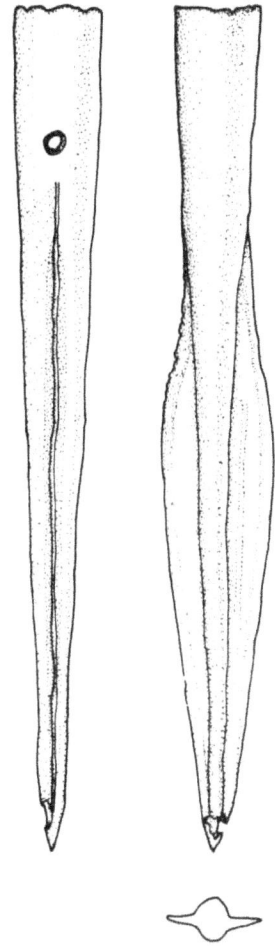

135

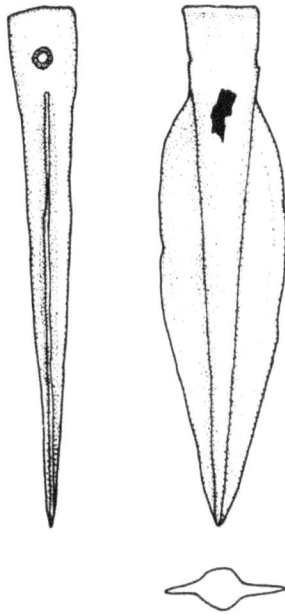

136

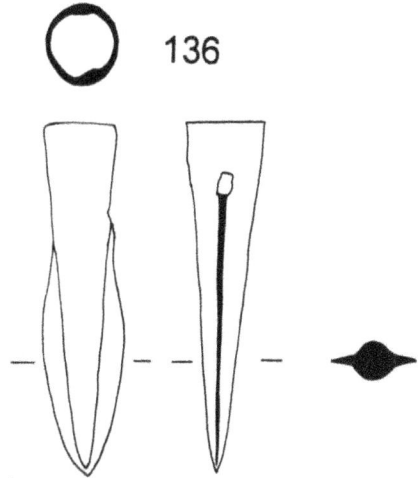

137

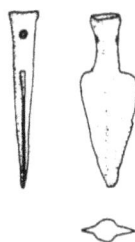

138

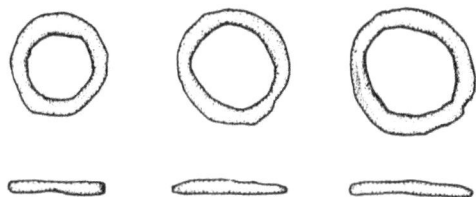

139 - 140 See plate IV

141

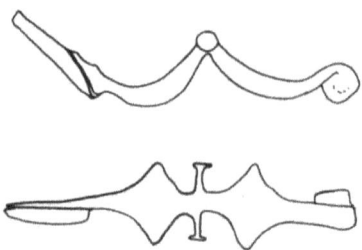

143

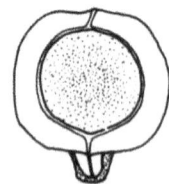

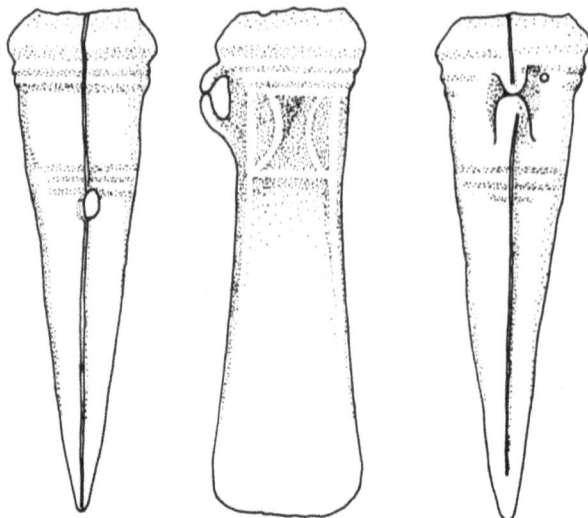

142

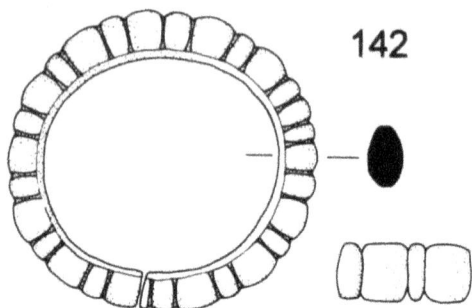

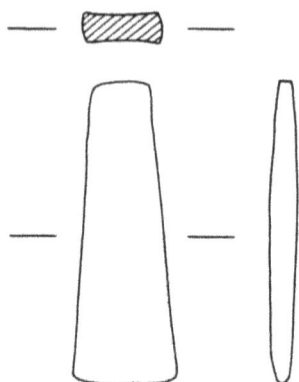

144

145

146

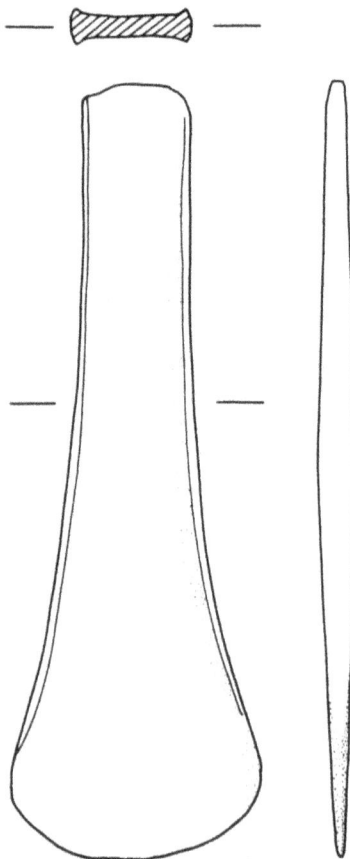

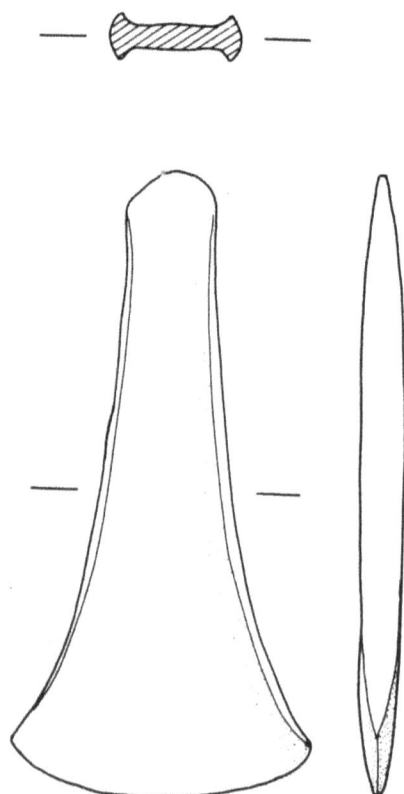

147

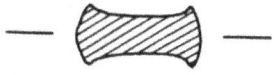

148

149

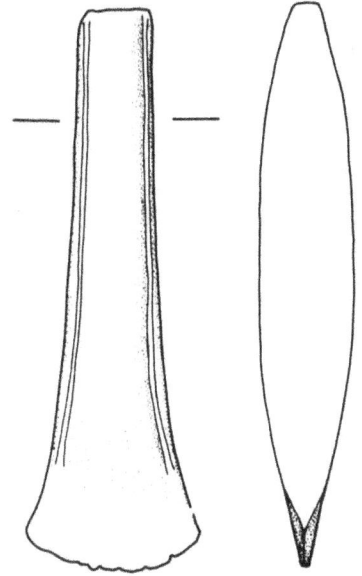

150

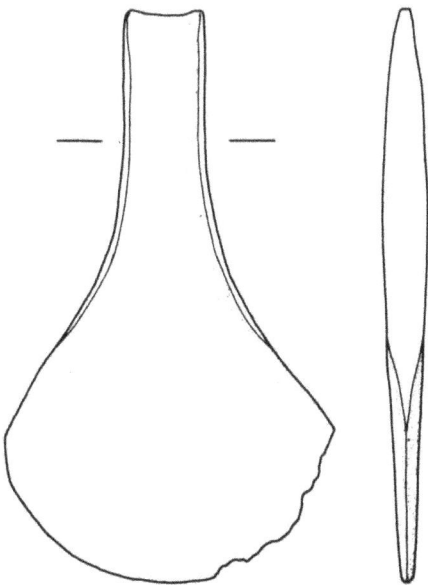

151

152

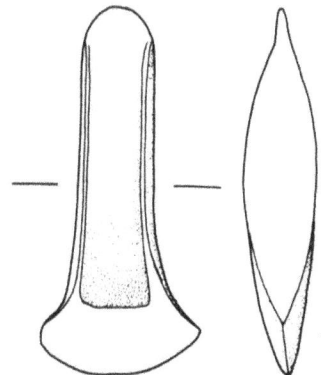

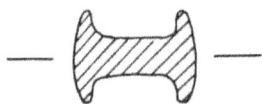

153

154

155

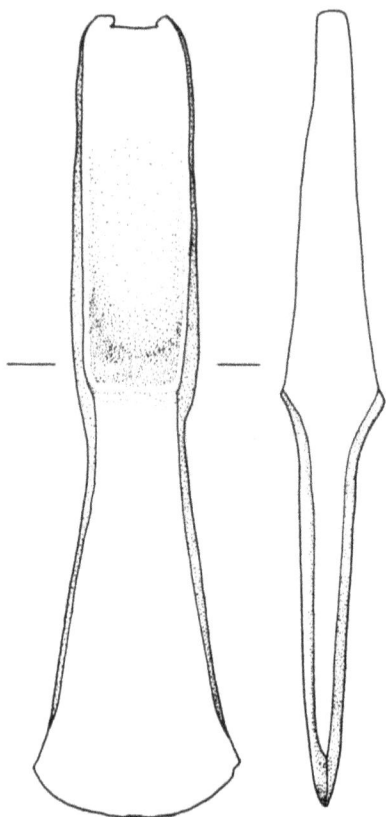

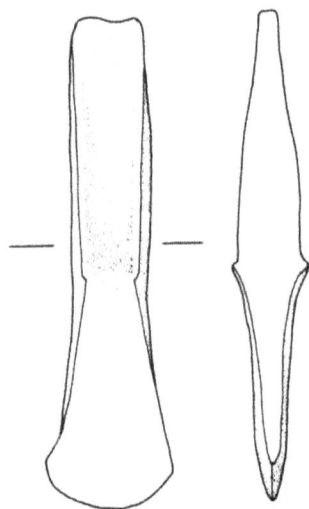

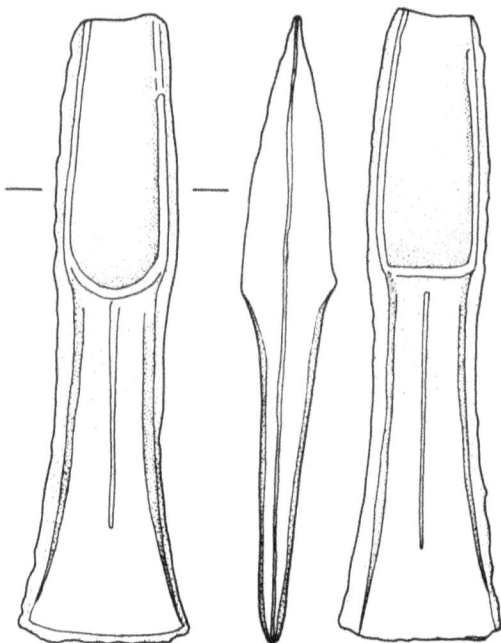

156

157

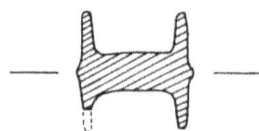

158

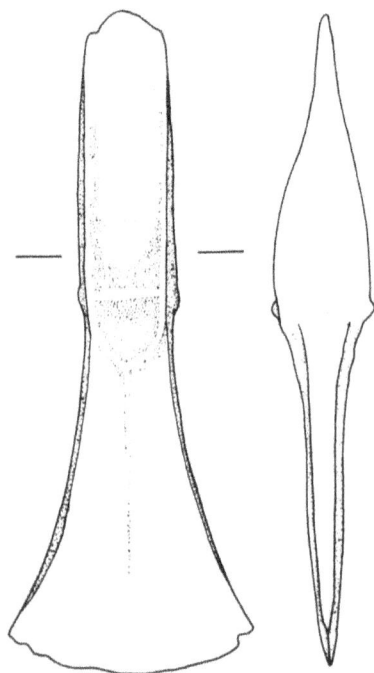

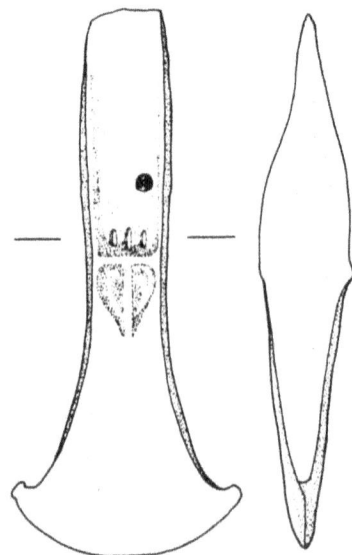

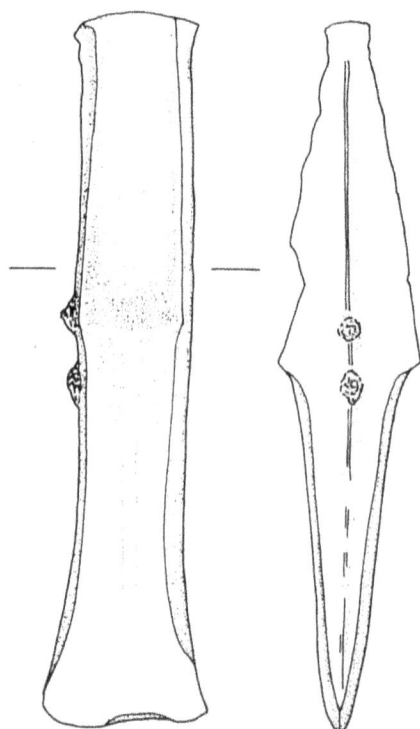

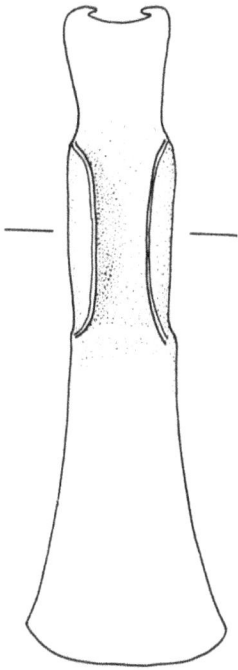

159

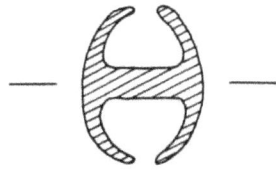
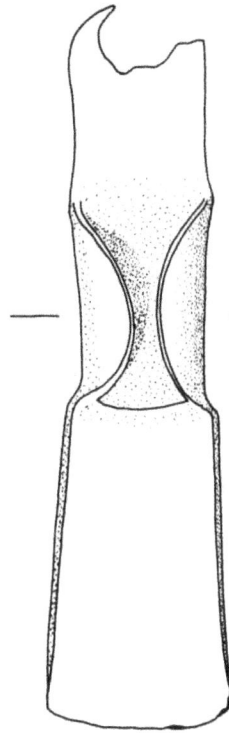
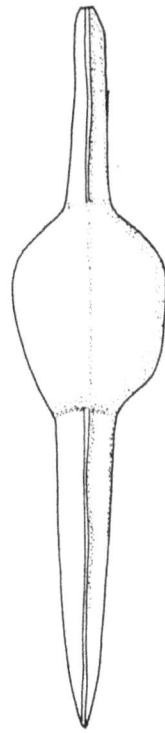

160

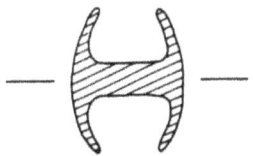
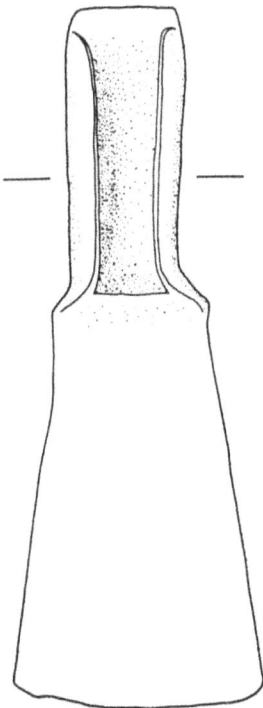
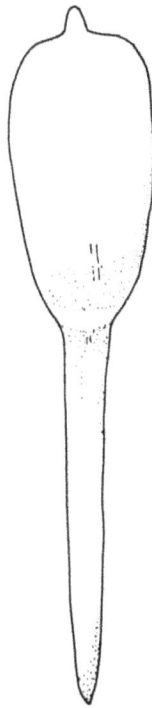

161

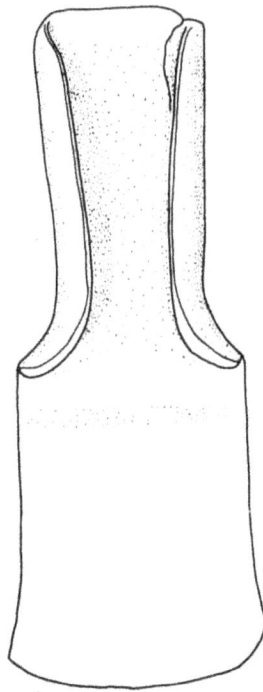
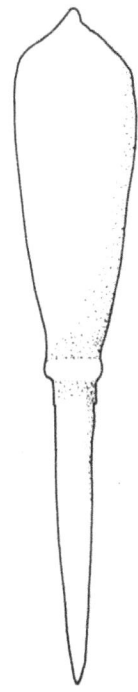

162

163

164
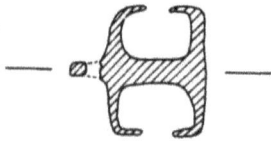

165

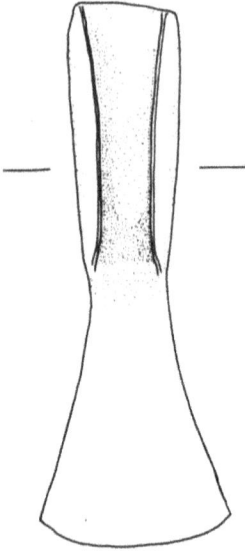

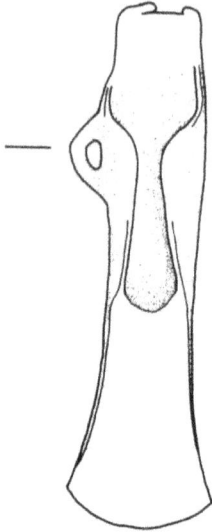

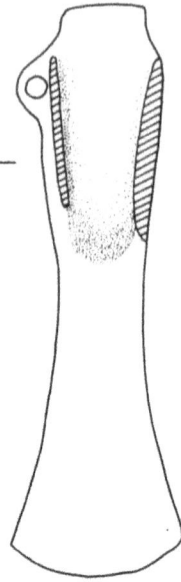
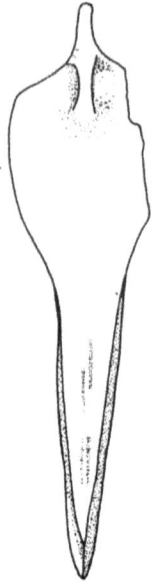

166
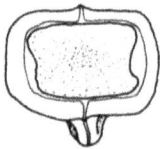
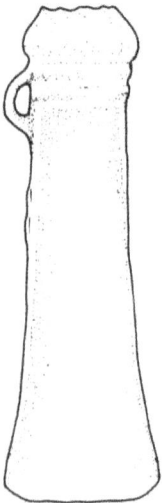
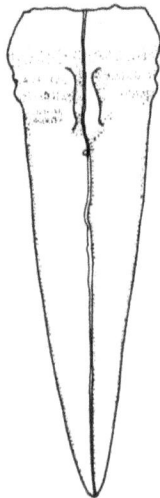

167
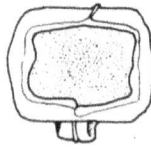
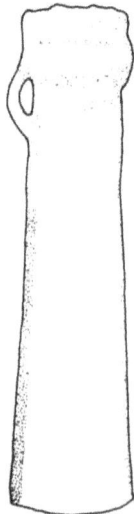
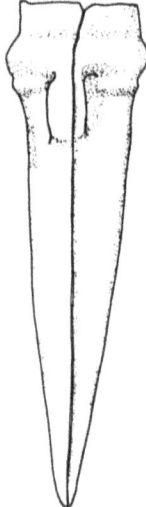

168

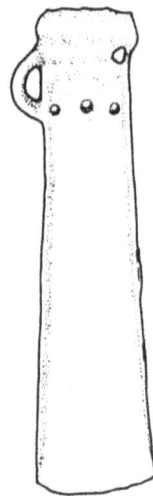
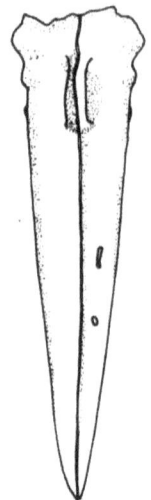

169

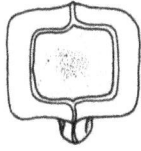 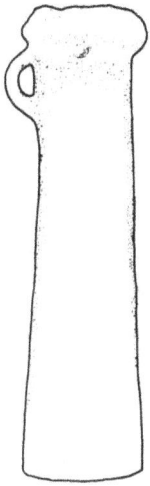 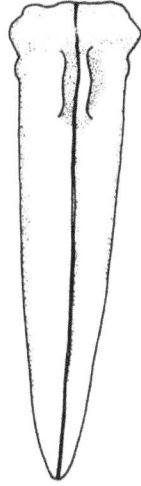

170

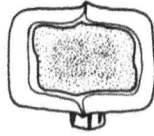  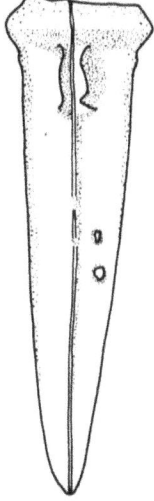

171

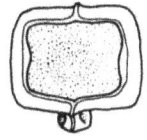 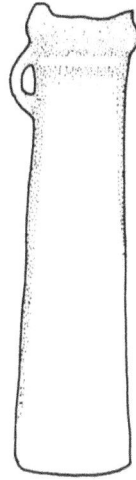 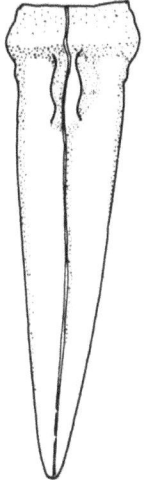

172

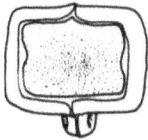 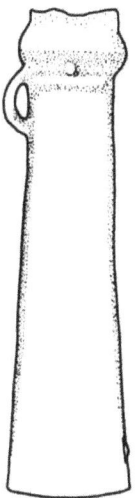 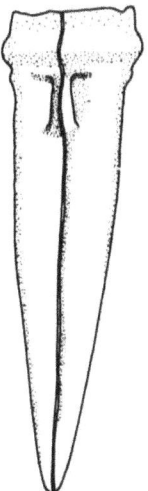

173

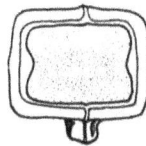  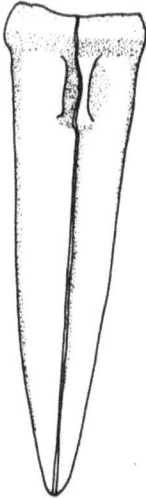

174

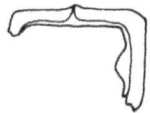  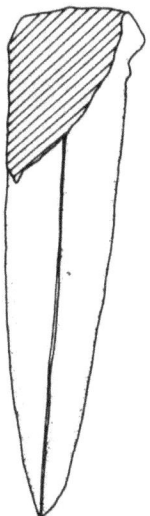

175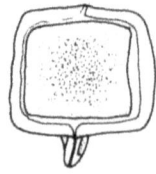

176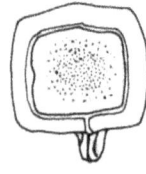

177

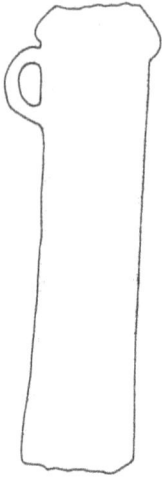 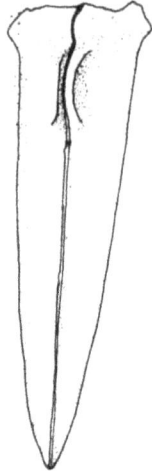 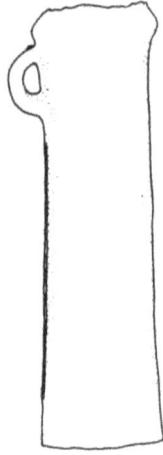  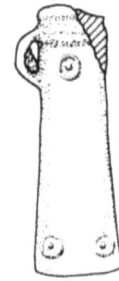 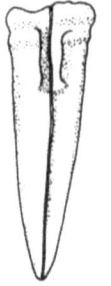

178 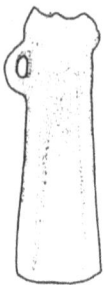 179   180    181

182  183   184

185 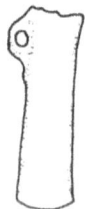  186

187

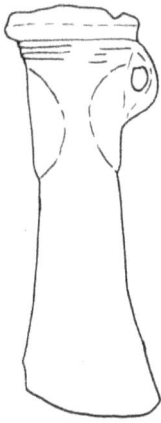 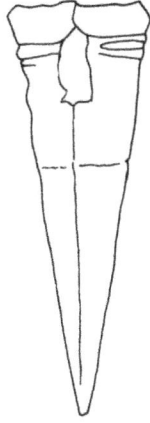

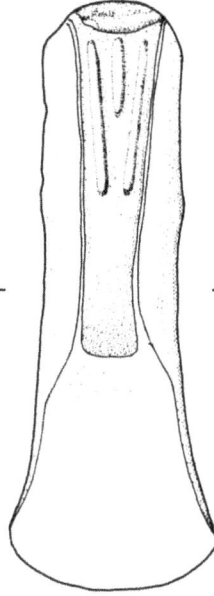 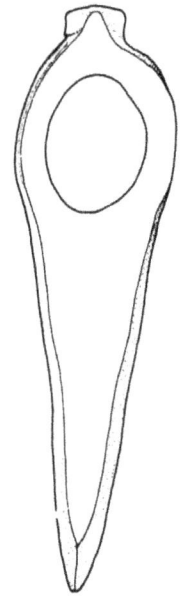

188

189

190

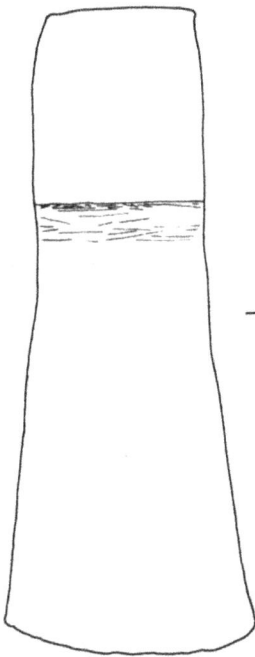 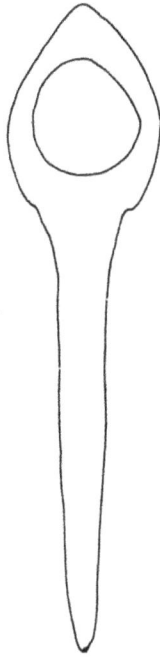

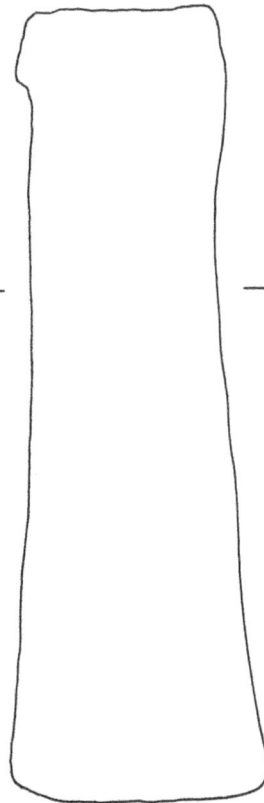 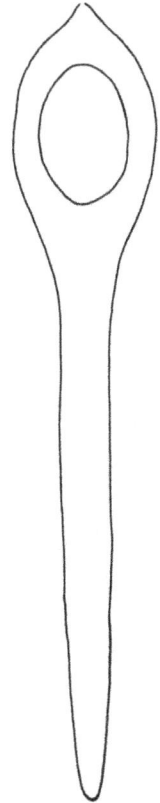

191

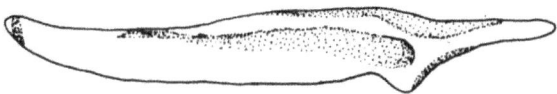

192 (1:4)   193 (1:4)   194 (1:4)   195

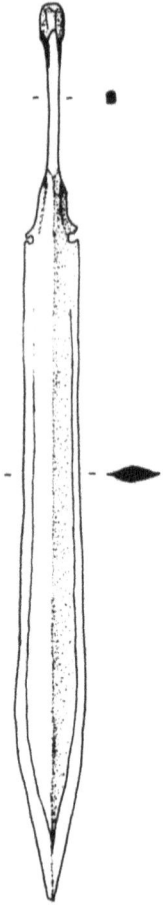
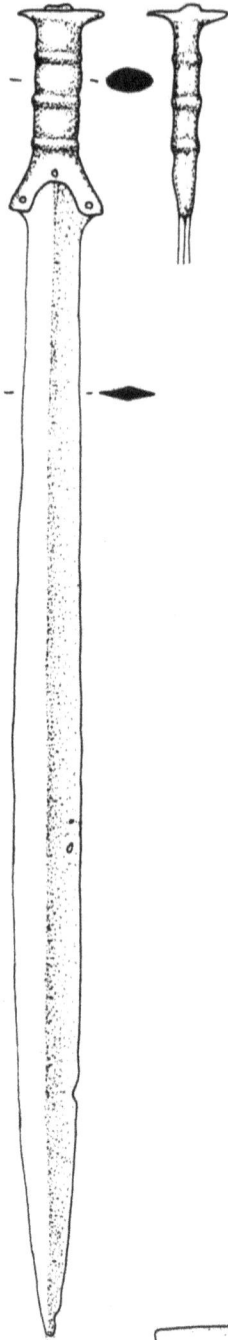
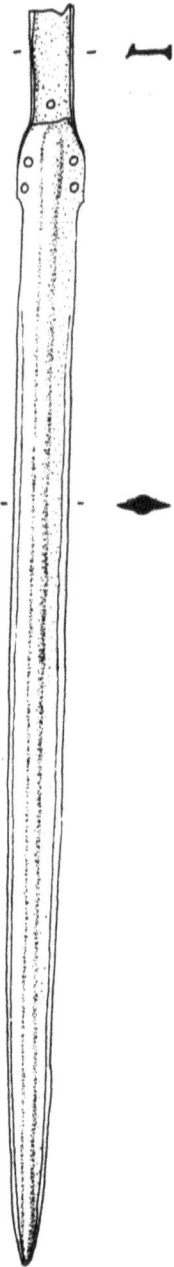
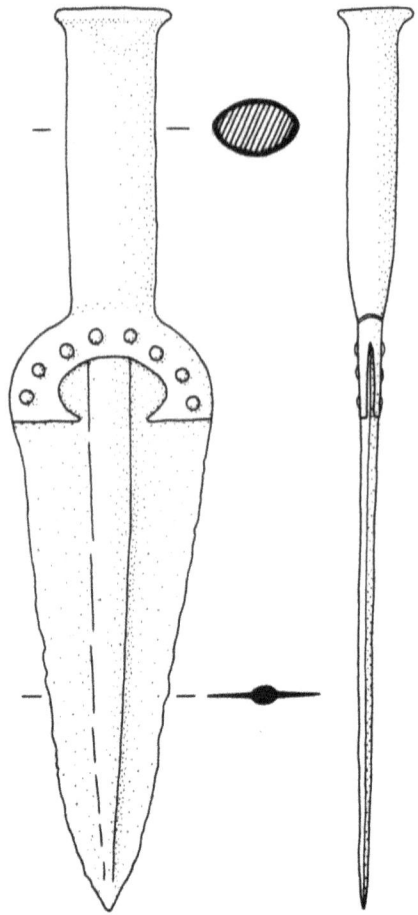

197

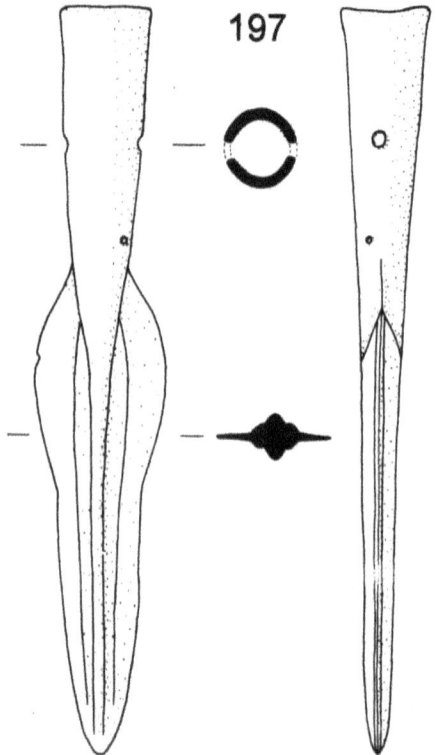

196

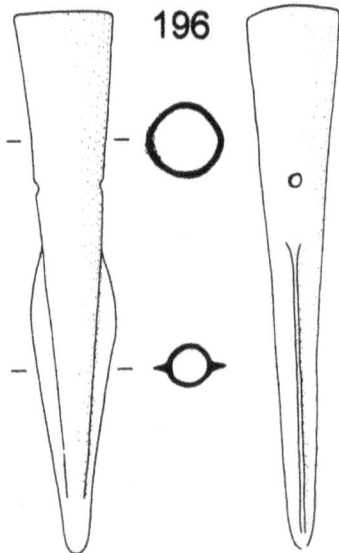

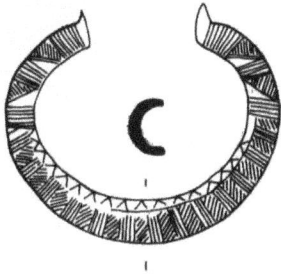

198

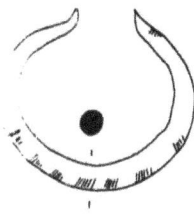

199

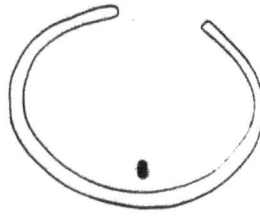

200

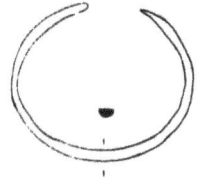

201

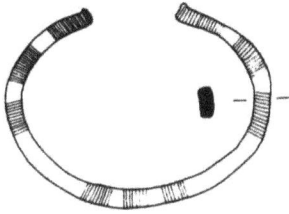

202

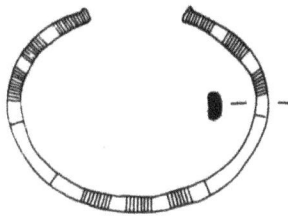

203

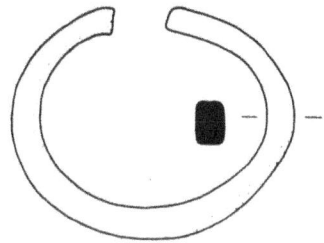

204

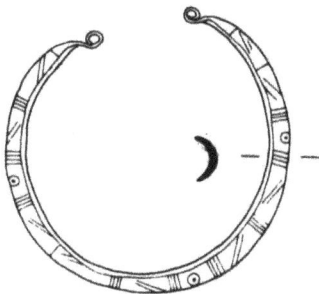

205

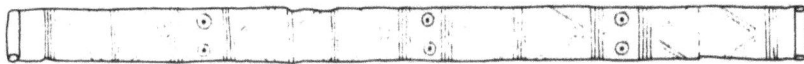

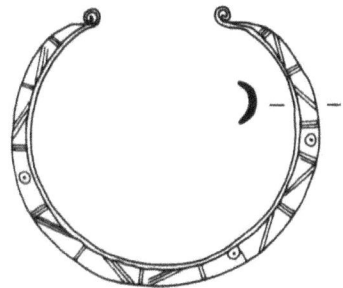

206

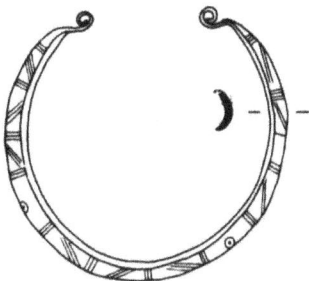

207

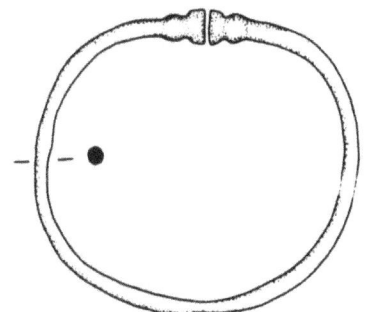

208

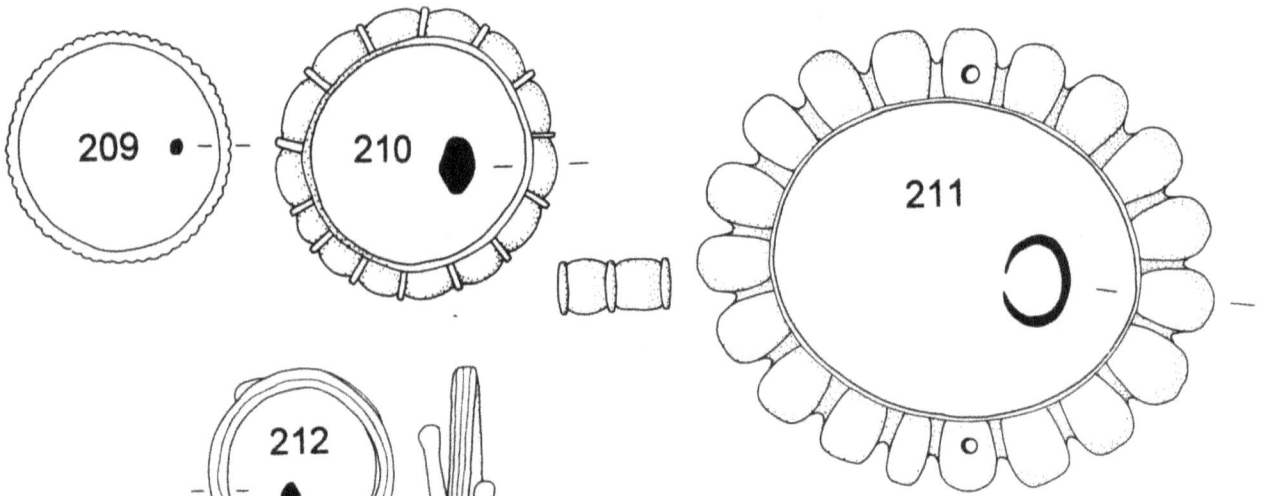

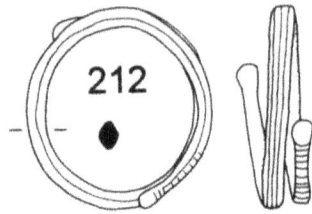

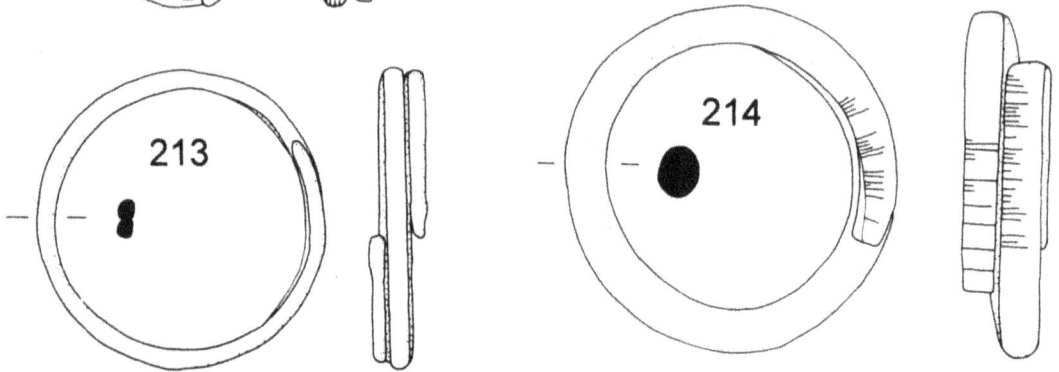

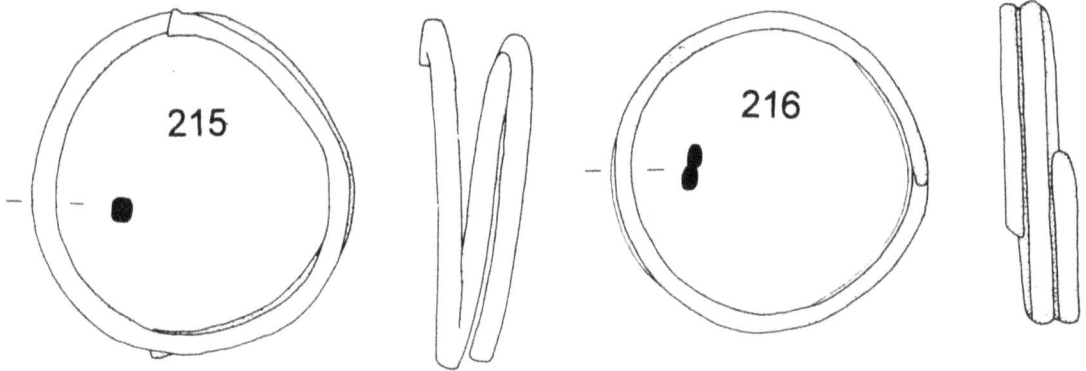

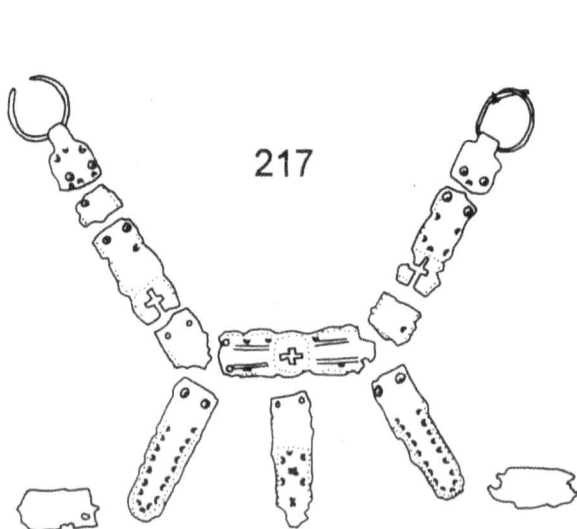

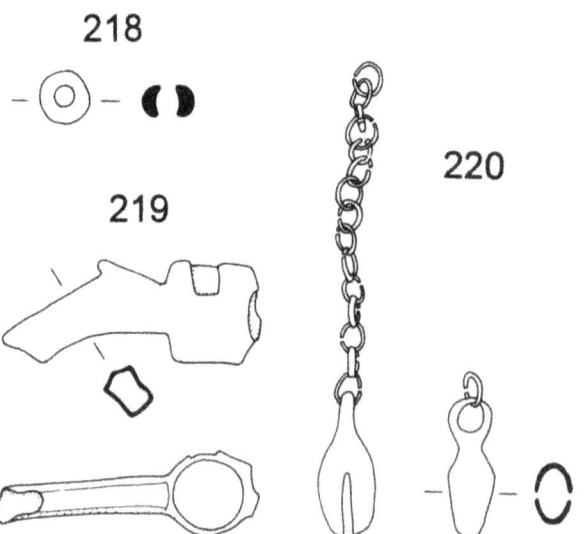

221

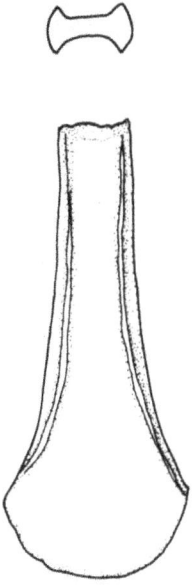

222

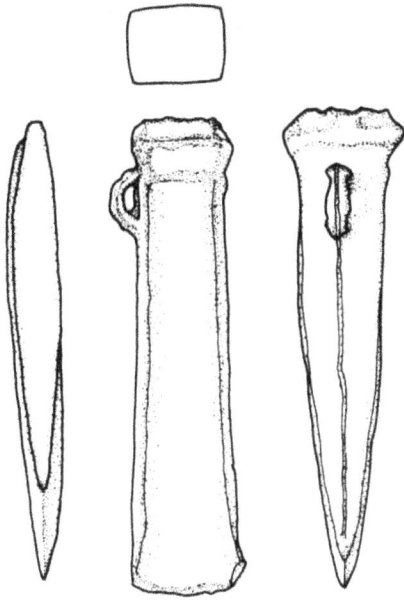

223

224

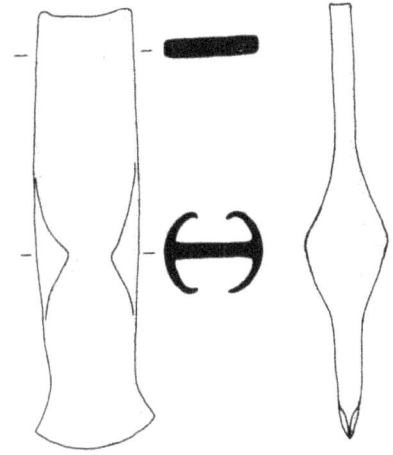

225

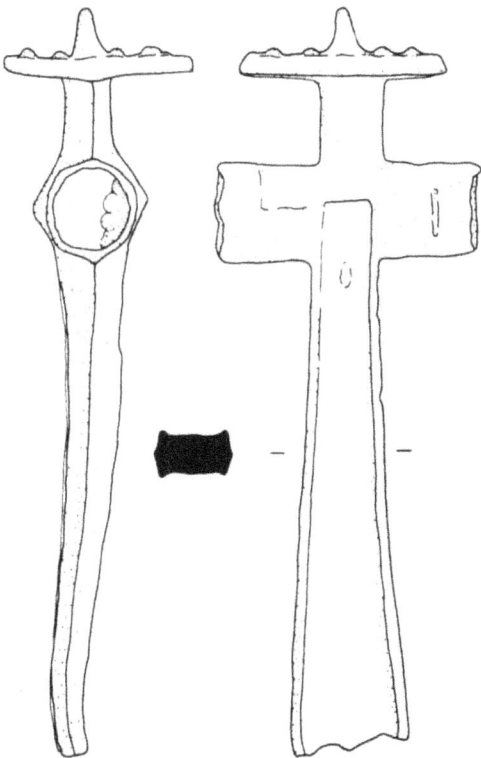

226

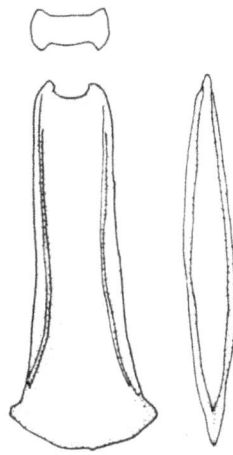

227

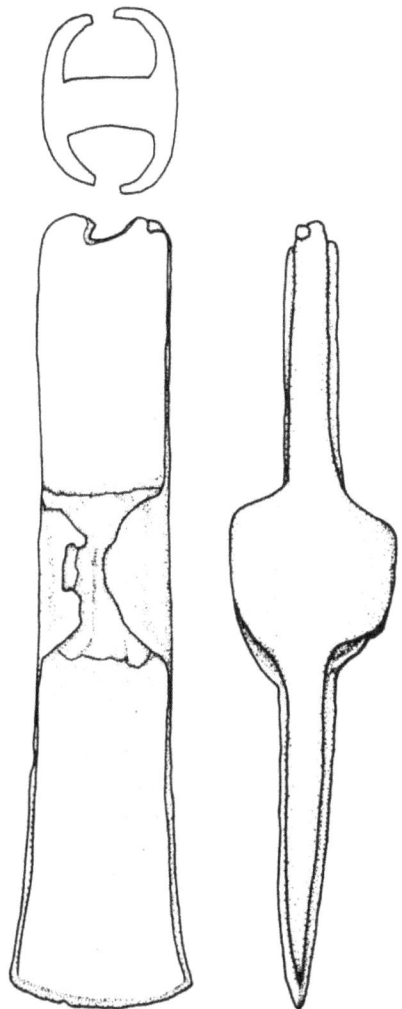

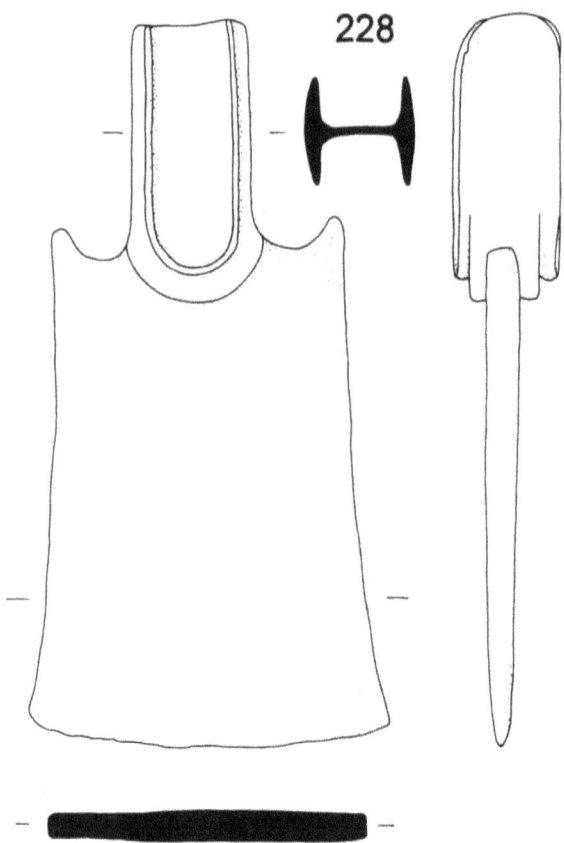

228

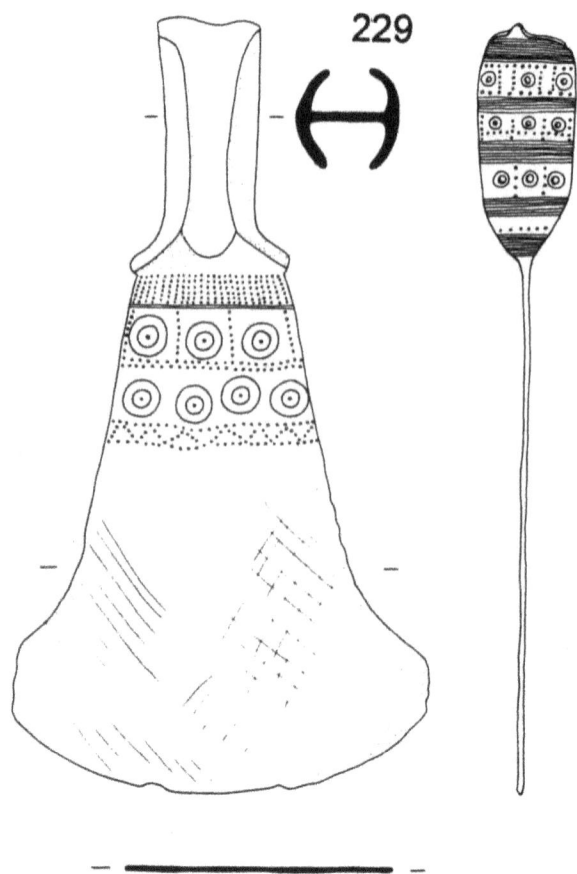

229

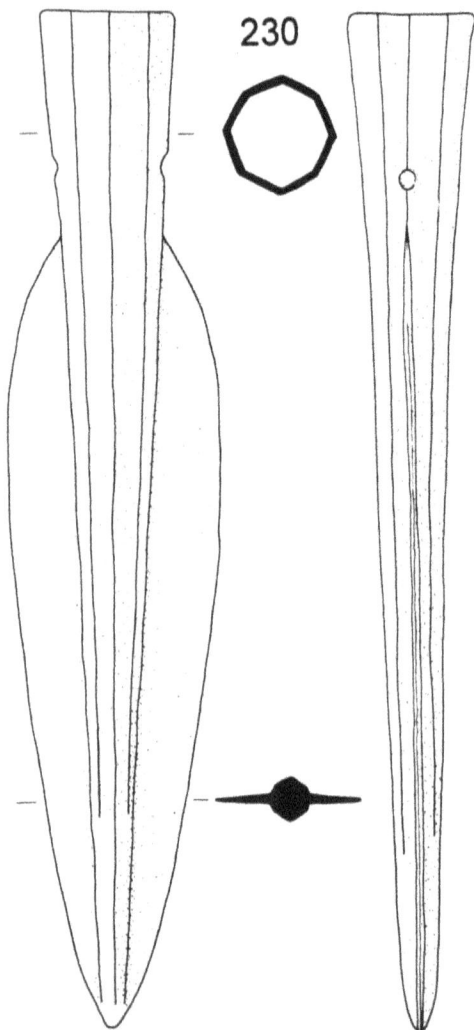

230

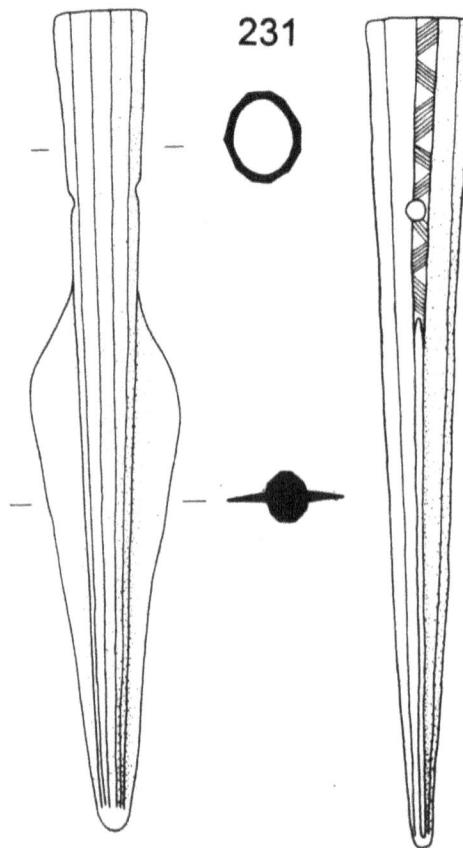

231

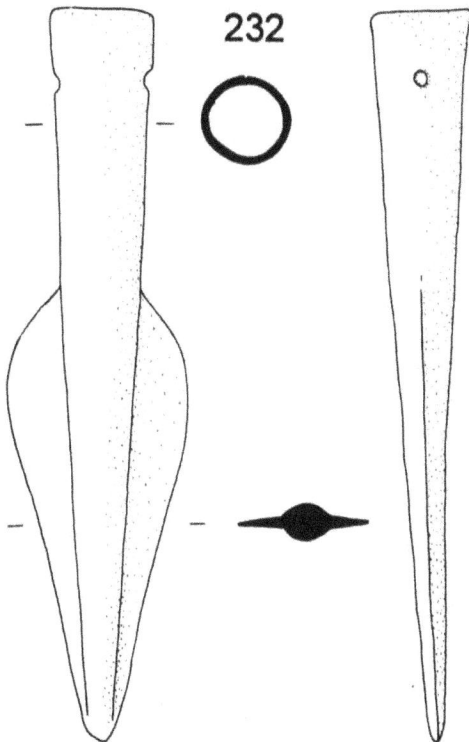

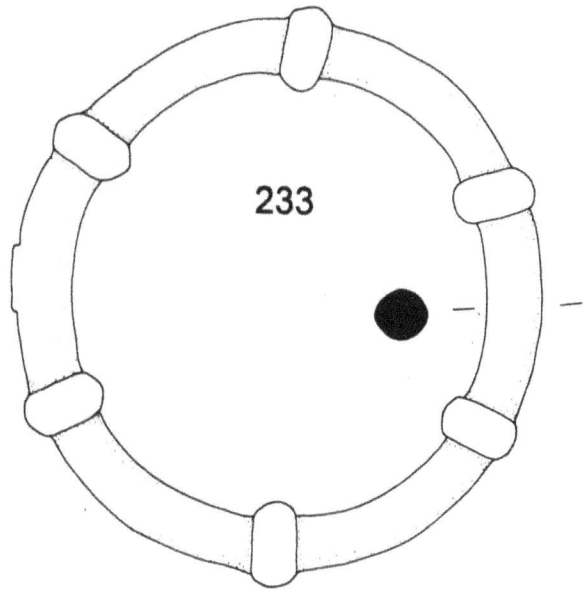

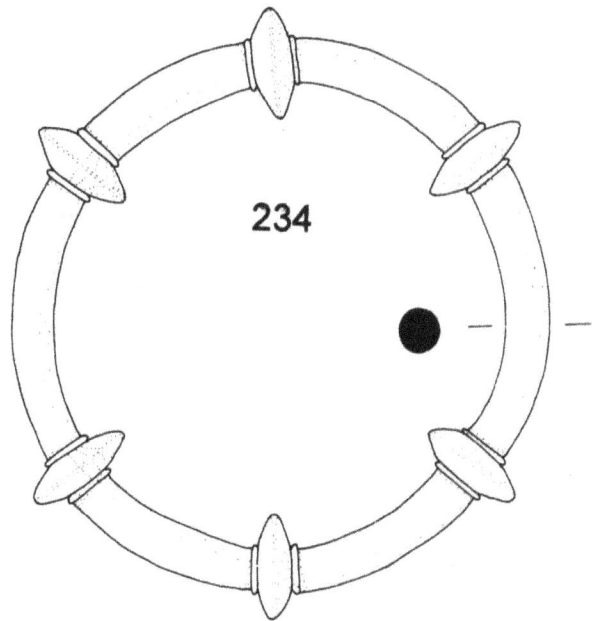

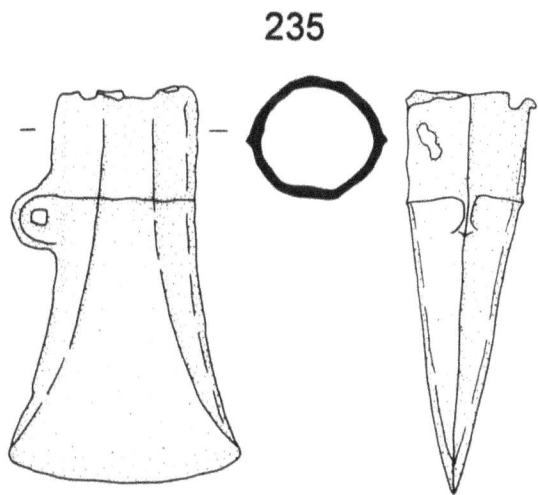

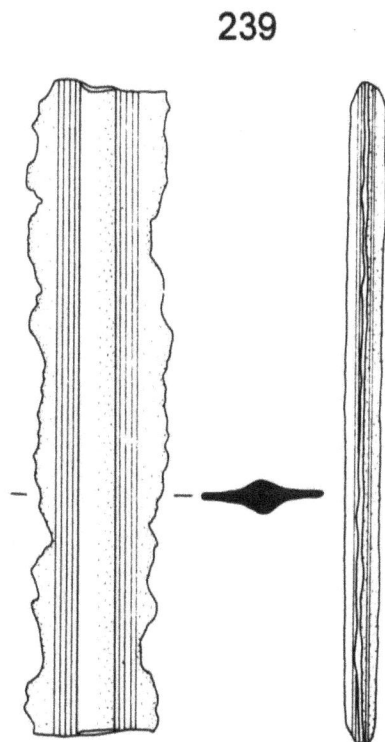

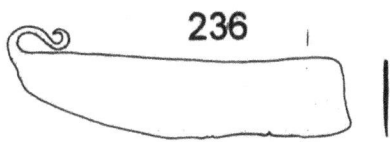

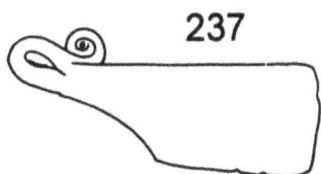

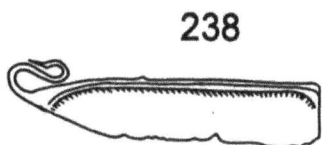

232

233

235

234

239

236

237

238

240

241

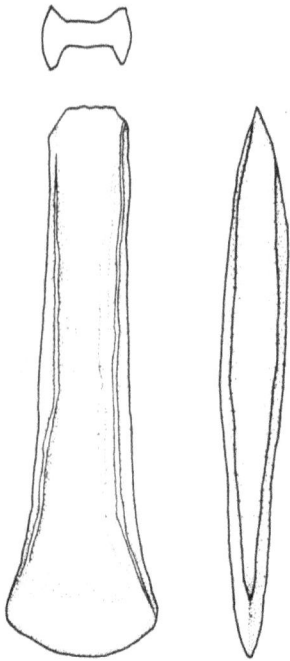

242

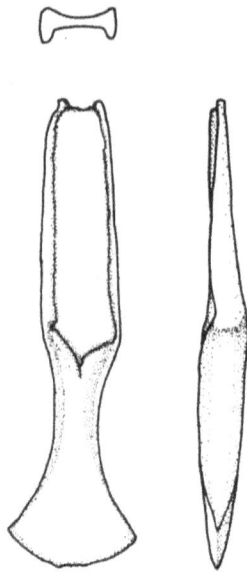

245

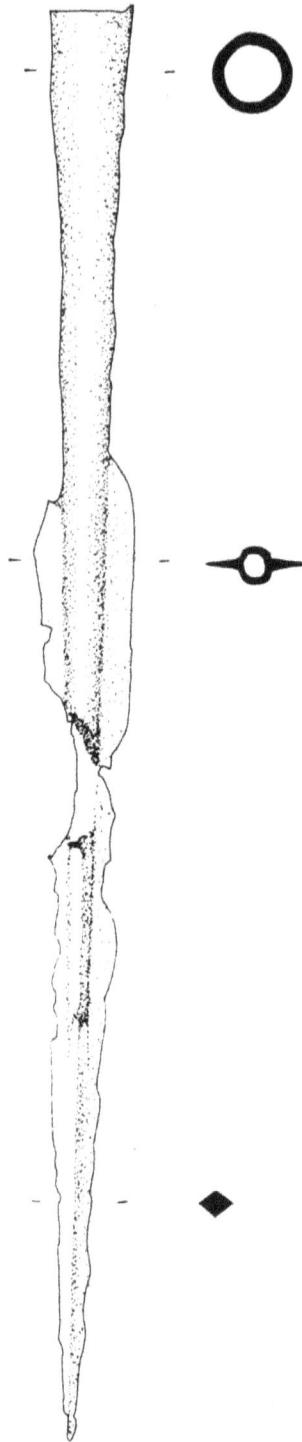

246

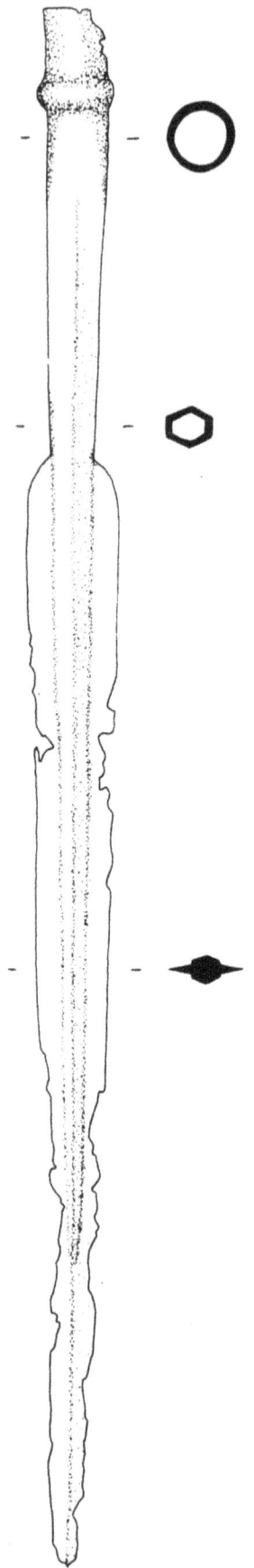

243

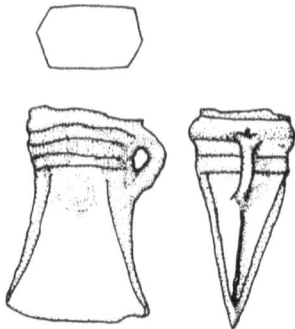

244
(1:4)

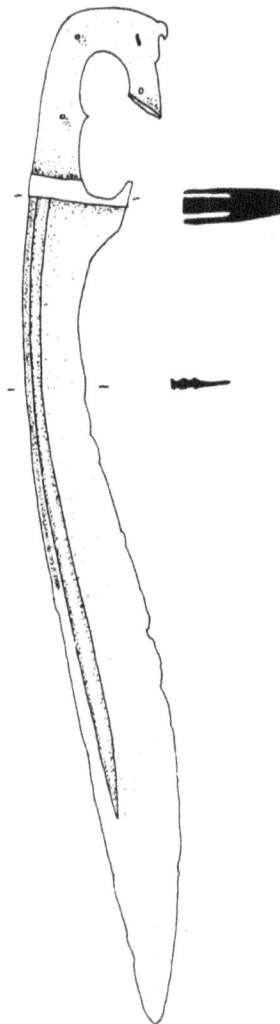

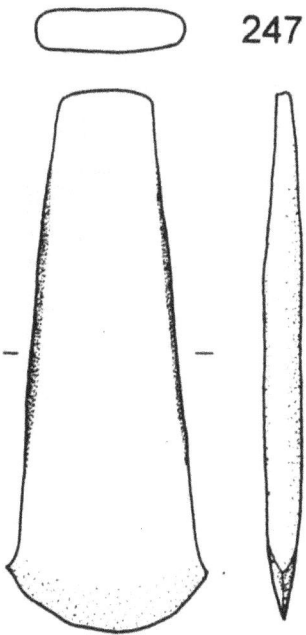

247

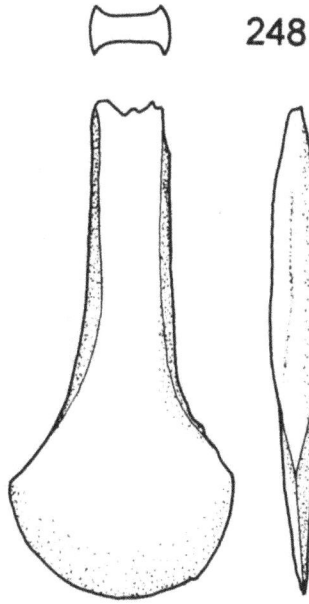

248

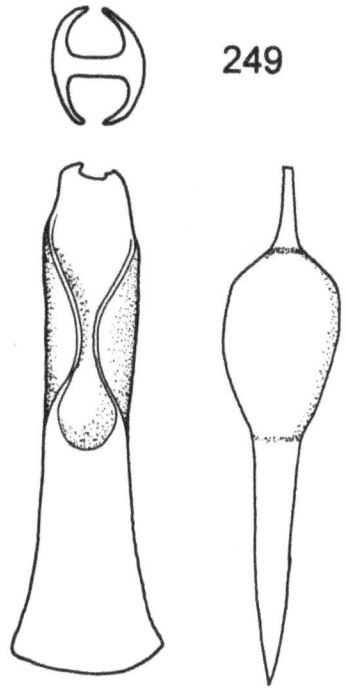

249

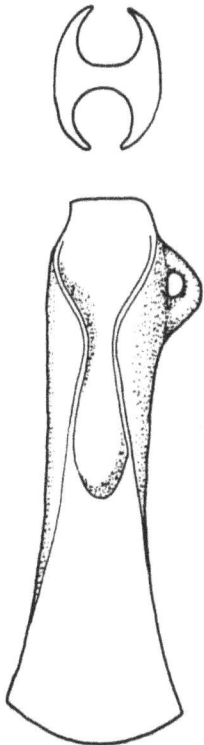

250

251

252

253

254

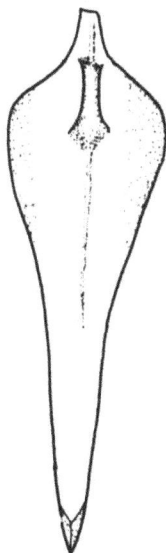

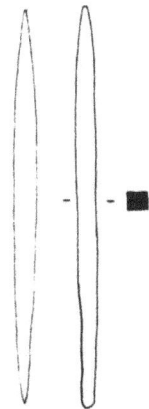

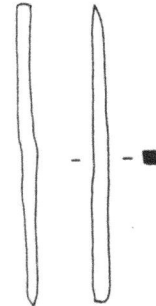

257 258 259

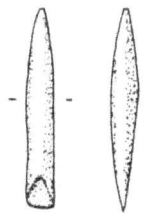

255

256

260 261 262 263

264

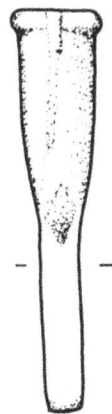

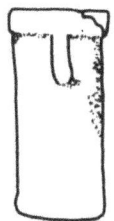

265

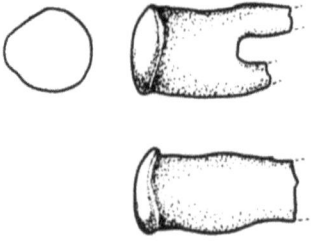

266

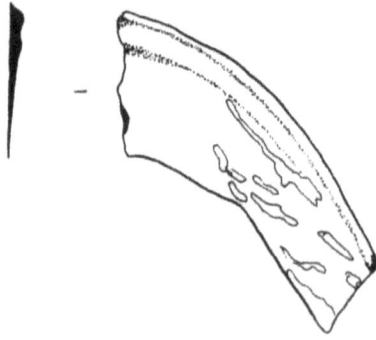

267

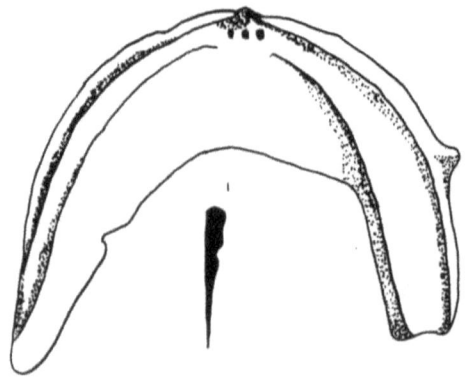

268

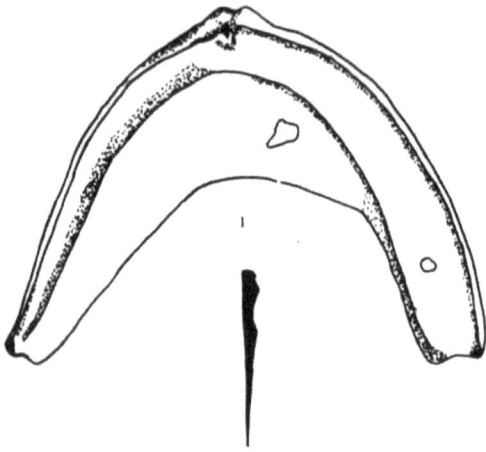

269

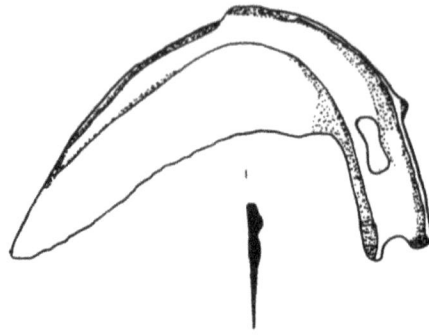

270

271

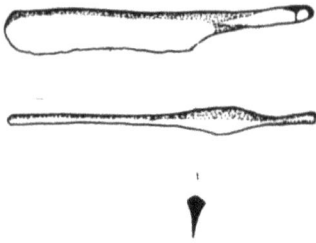

273

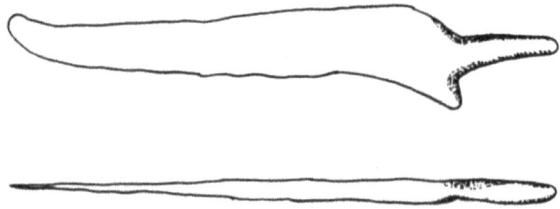

272

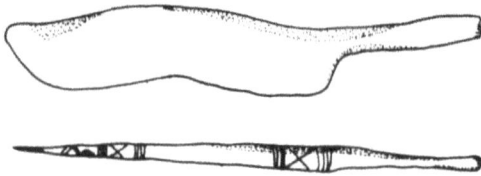

274

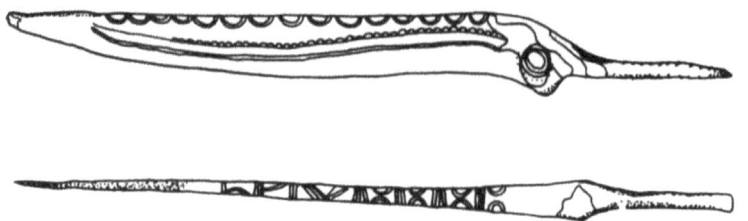

275

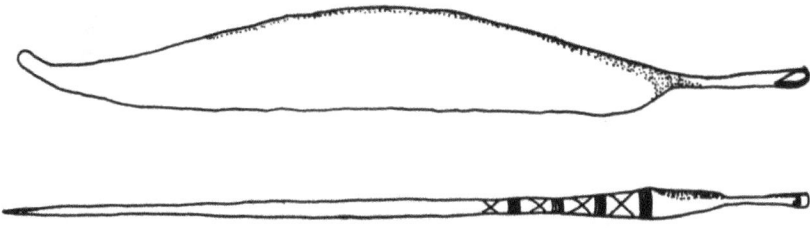

276

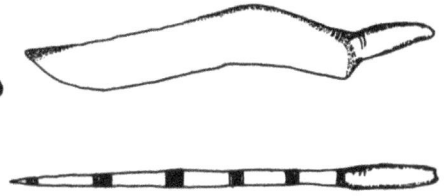

277

278

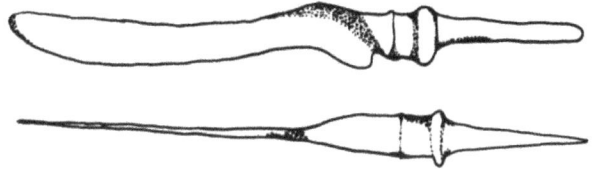

279

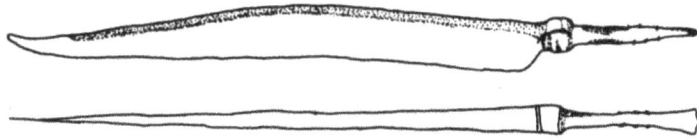

280

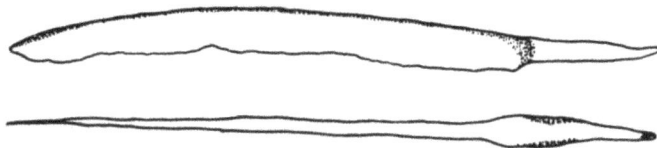

281

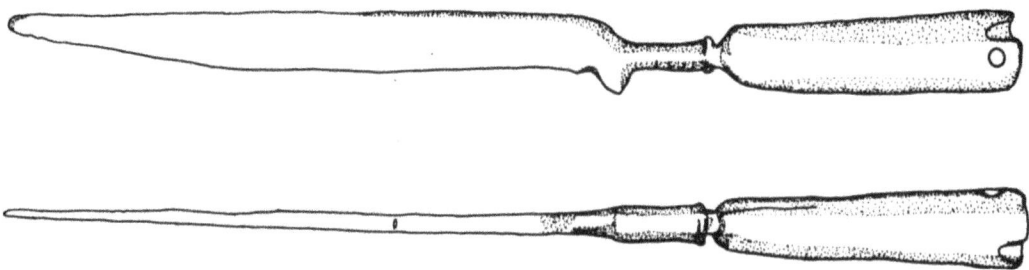

282

283

284

286

285

287

288 289 290 291 292 293 294 295 296 297 298 299 300

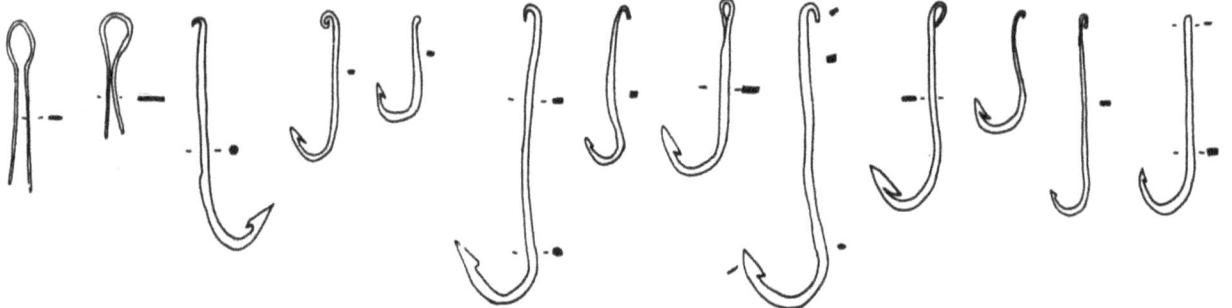

301 302 303 304 305 306 307 308 309 310 311 312 313 314

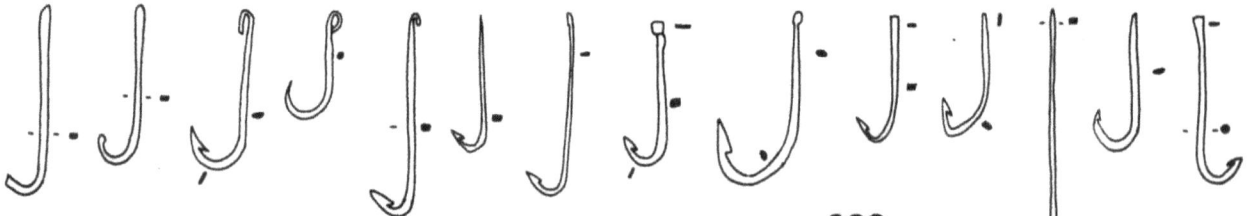

315 316 317 318 319 320 321 322

323

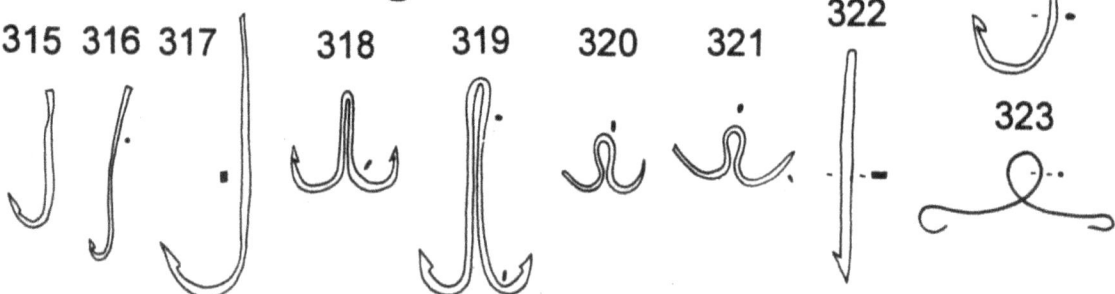

324   325   326 327   328 329   330

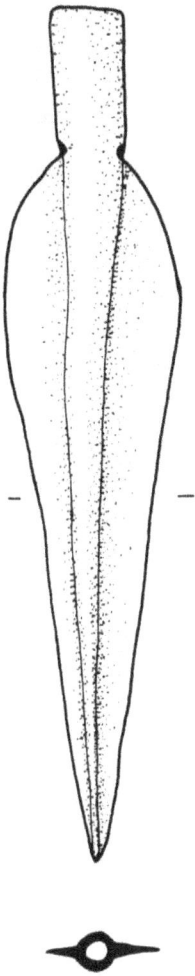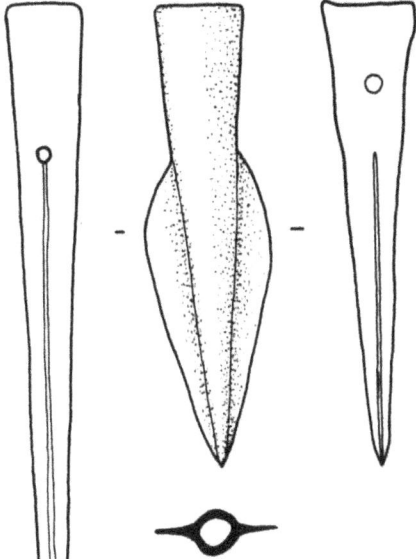

331 332 333 334 335 336

337 338 339 340 341

351

342 343 344 345 346   347   348 349   350

352 353 354 355 356

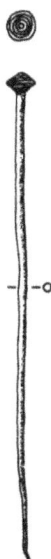

357 358 359 360 361 362 363 364 365 366 367 368 369 370 371

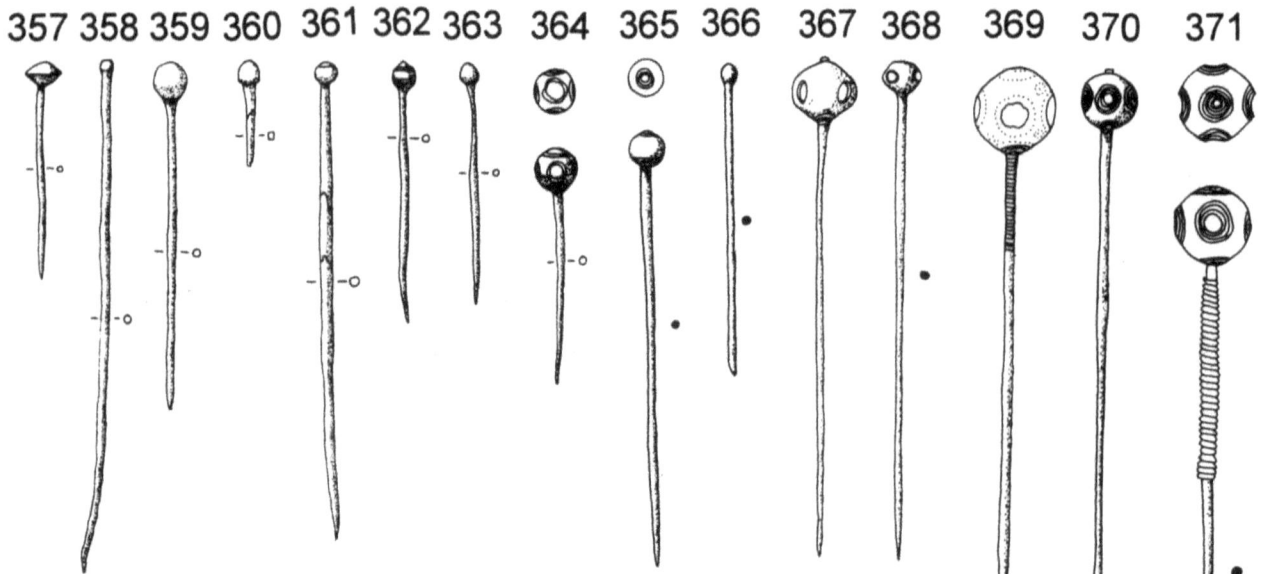

372 373 374 375 376 377 378 379

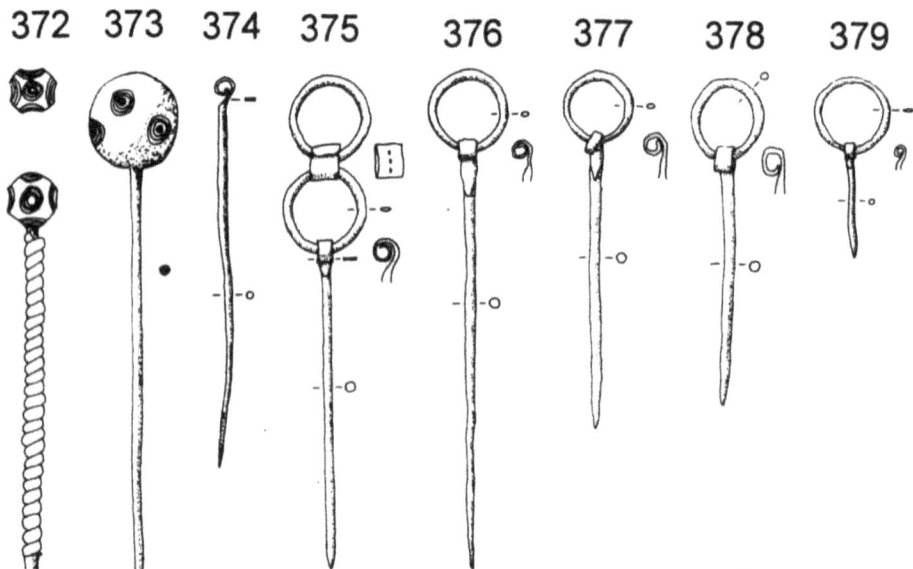

380 381 382 383 384 385 386 387 388

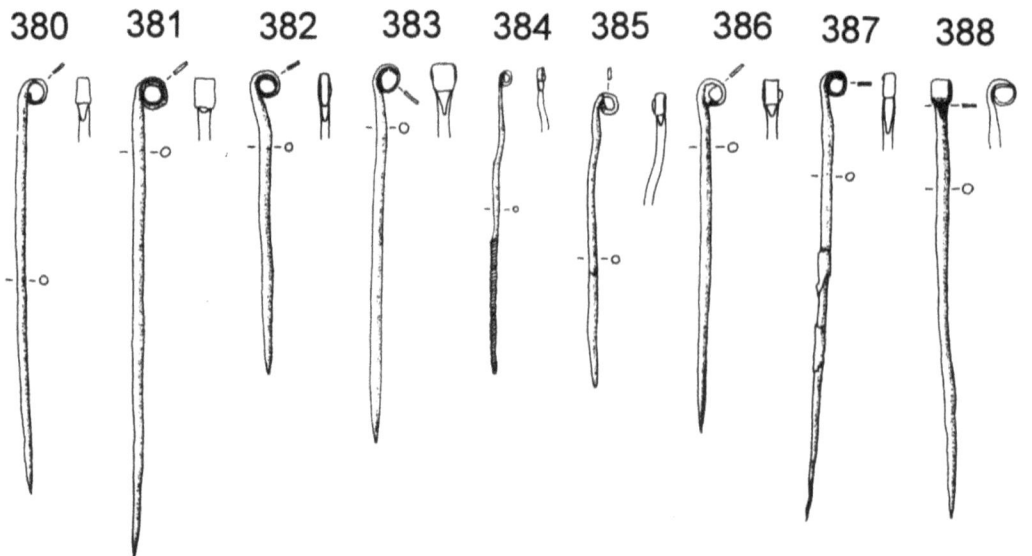

389 390 391 392 393 394 395 396 397 398 399 400 401 402

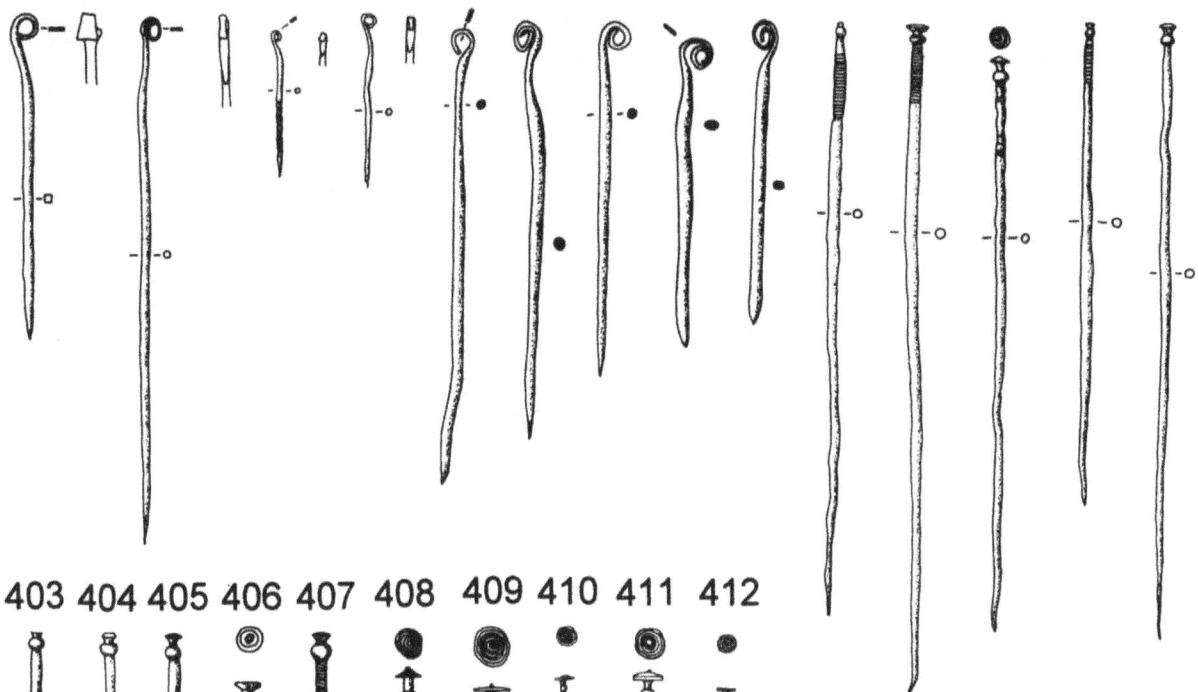

403 404 405 406 407 408 409 410 411 412

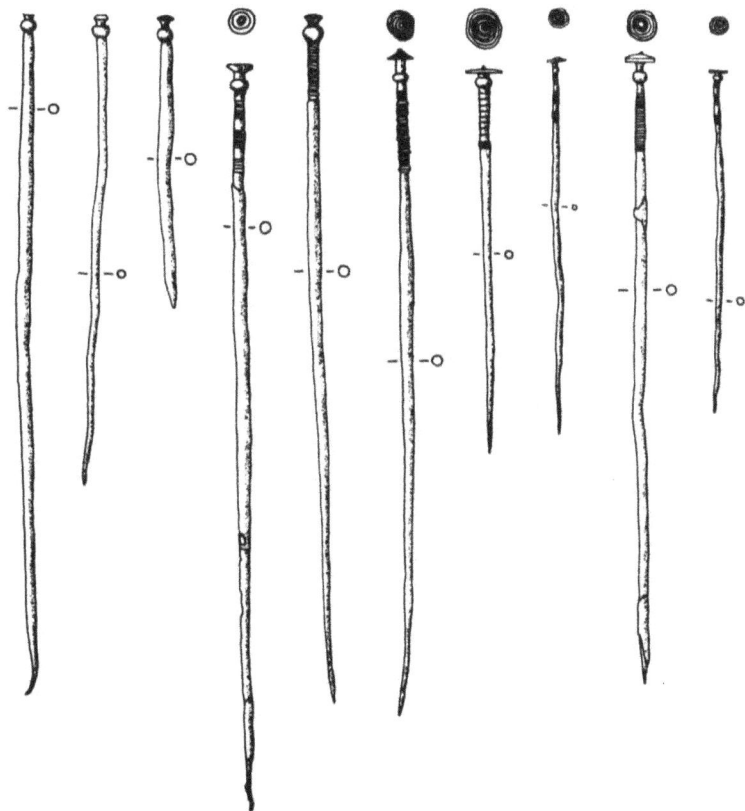

413 414 415 416 417 418

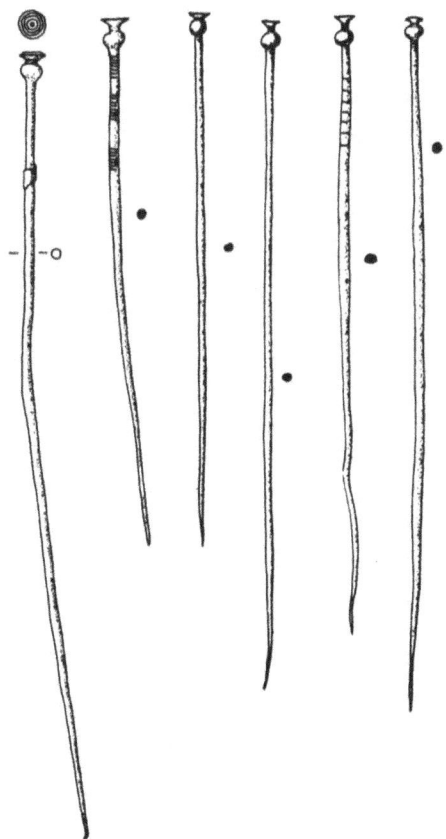

419 420 421 422 423 424 425 426 427 428 429 430 431 432

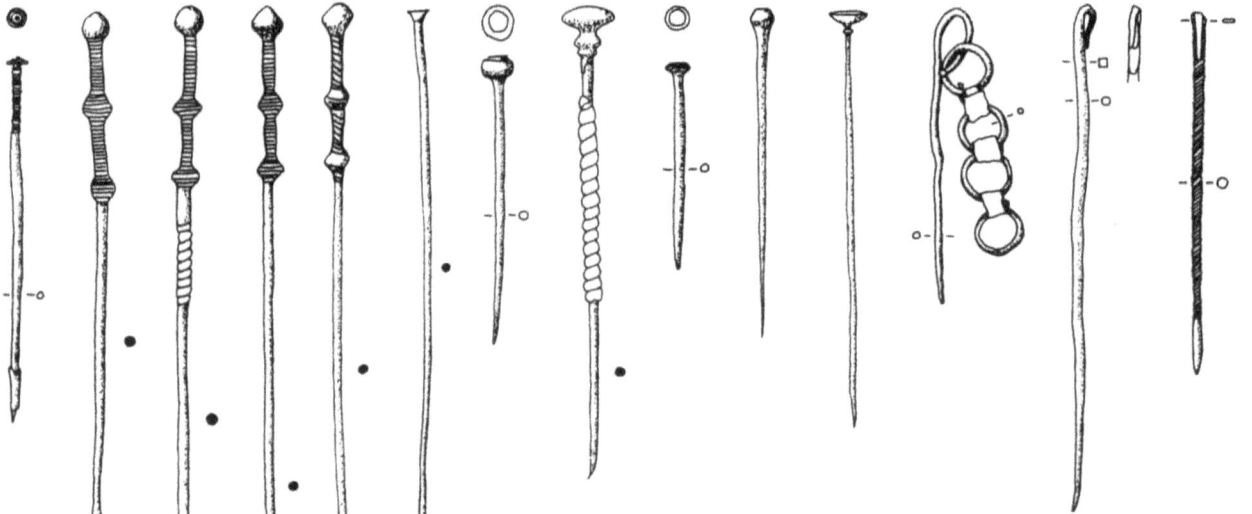

435

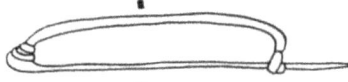

436

437

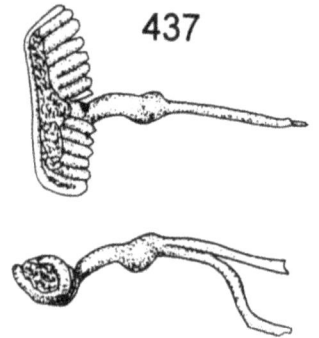

433 434 438 439

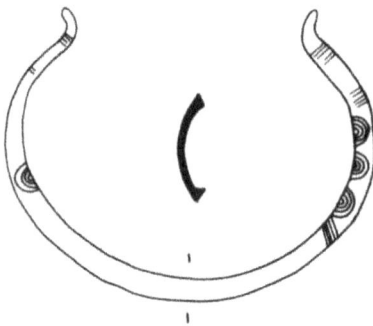

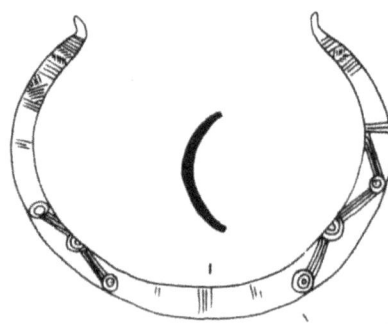

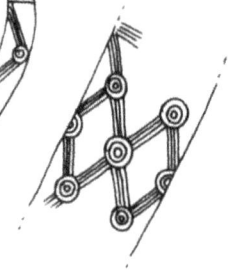

440 441 442 443 444 445 446

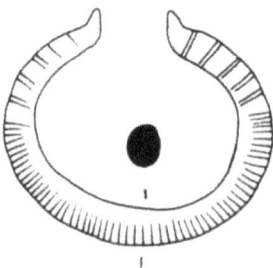

447 448 449 450 451

452 453 454 455 456 457

458 459 460 461 462

463 464 465

466 467 468 469 470

471 472 473 474

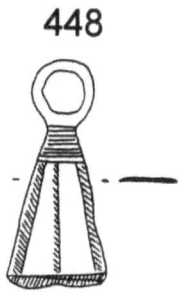

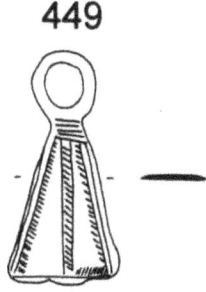

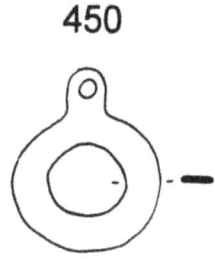

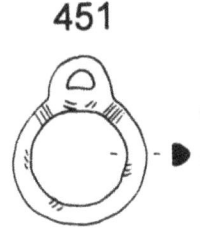

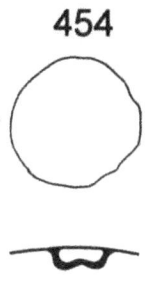

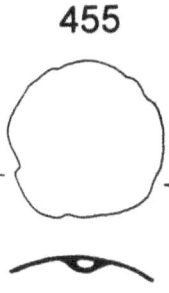

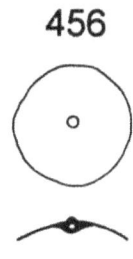

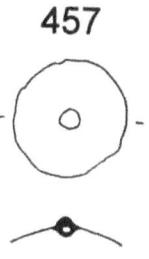

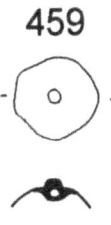

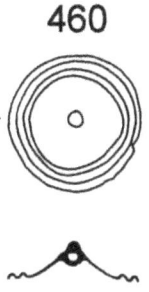

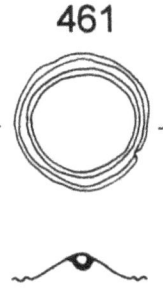

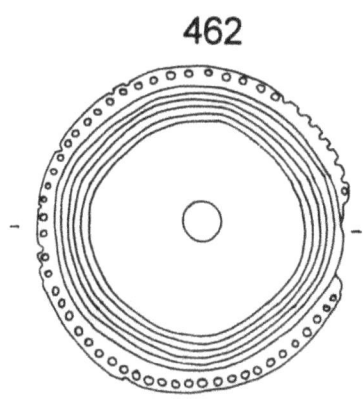

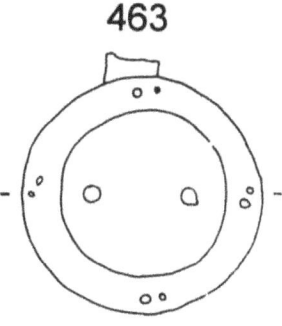

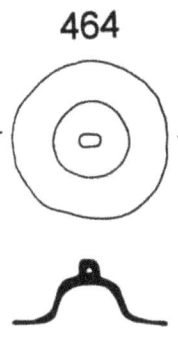

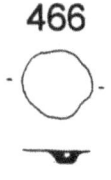

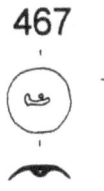

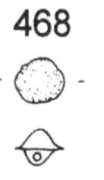

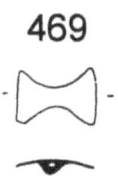

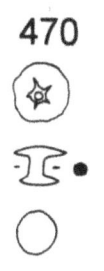

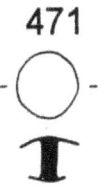

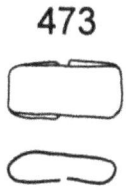

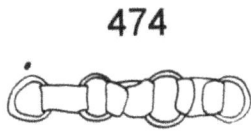

475 - 478
not
illustrated

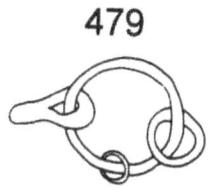

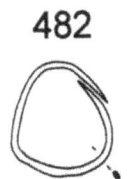

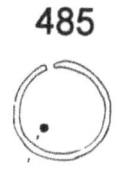

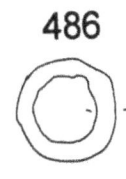

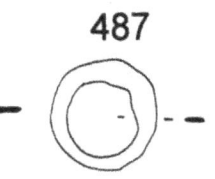

479

480 481 482 483 484 485 486 487

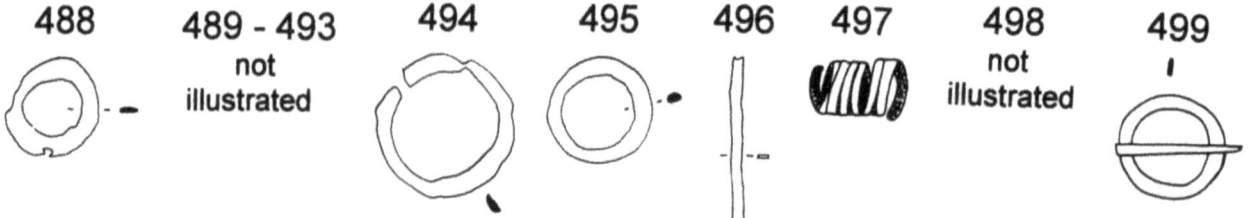

488 489 - 493
not
illustrated 494 495 496 497 498
not
illustrated 499

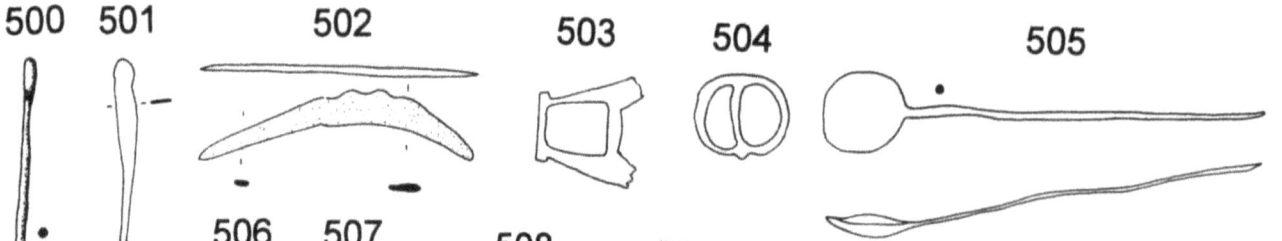

500 501 502 503 504 505

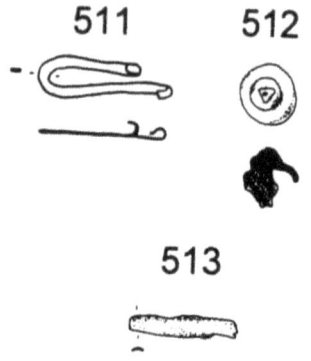

506 507 508 509 510 511 512

513

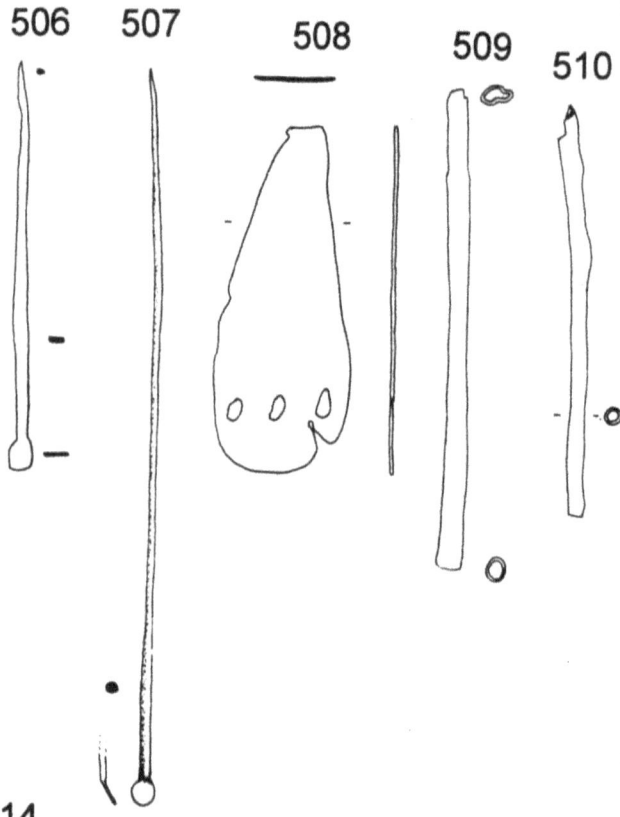

514 515

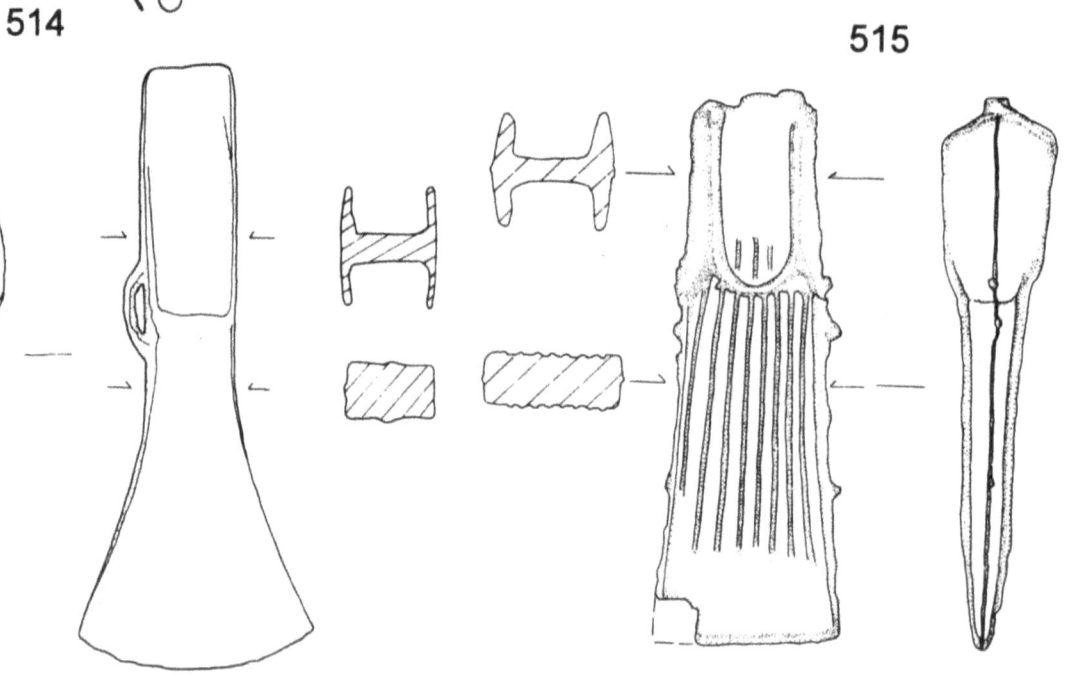

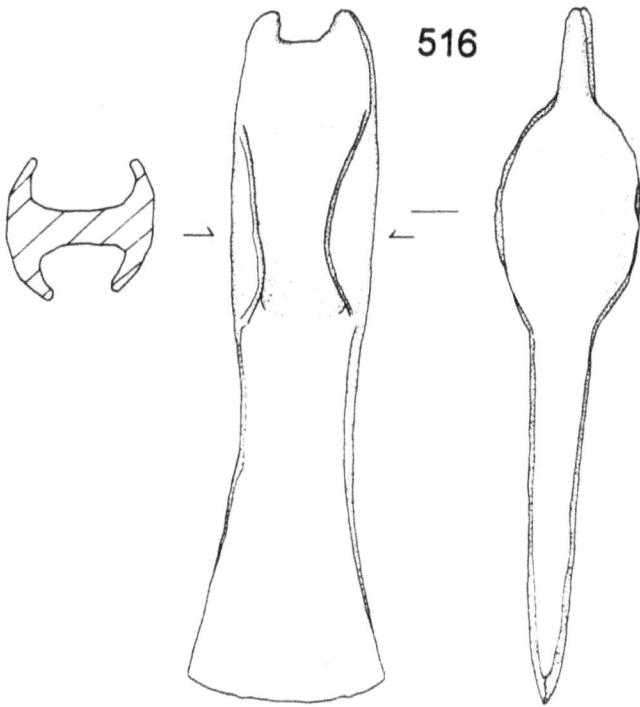

516

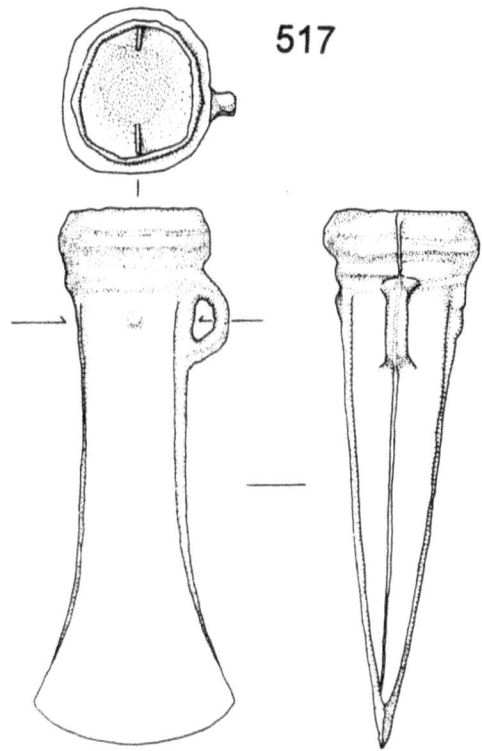

517

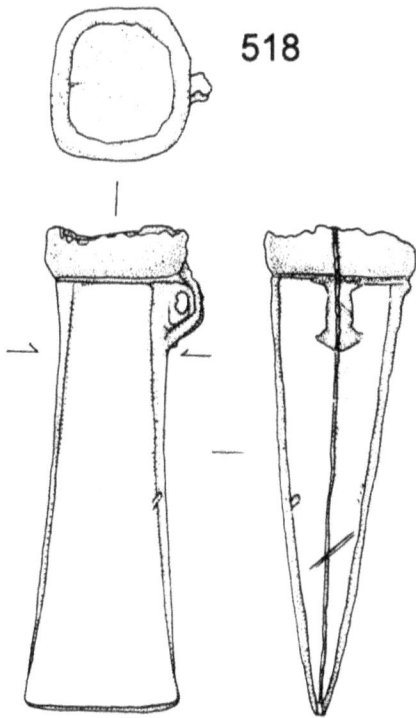

518

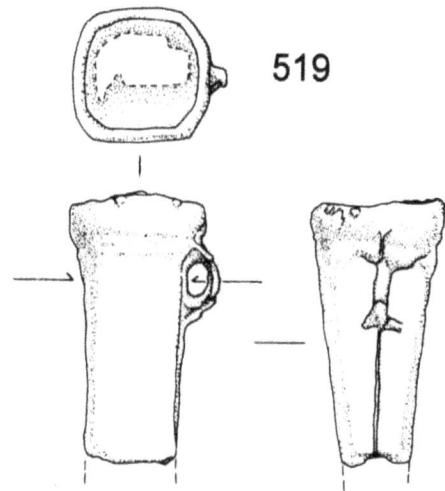

519

521

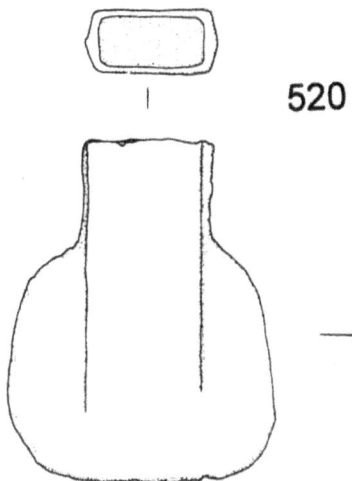

520

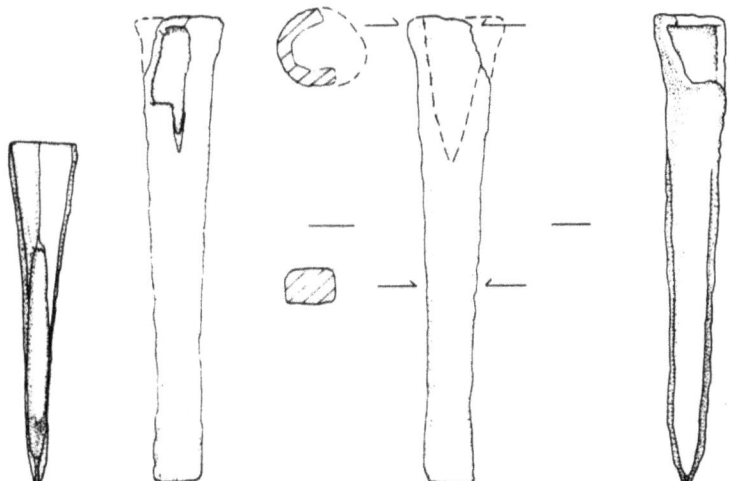

522

523

524

525

526

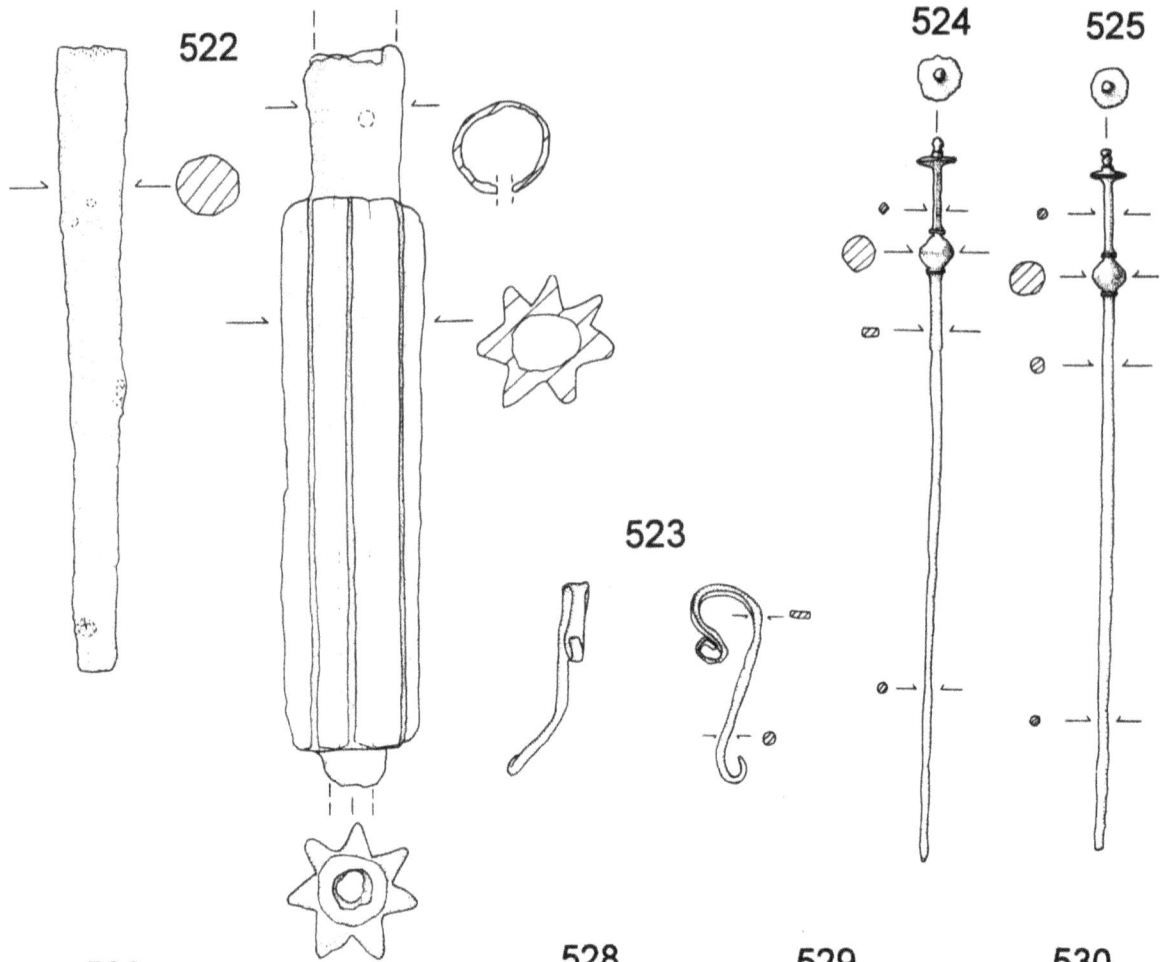

527
see
plate V

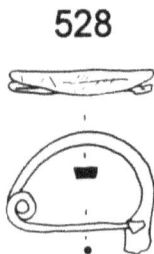

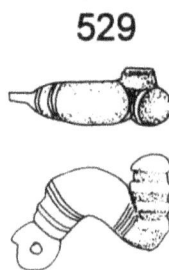

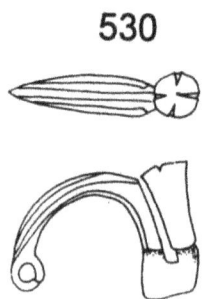

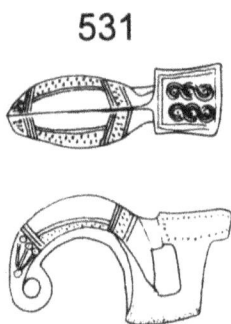

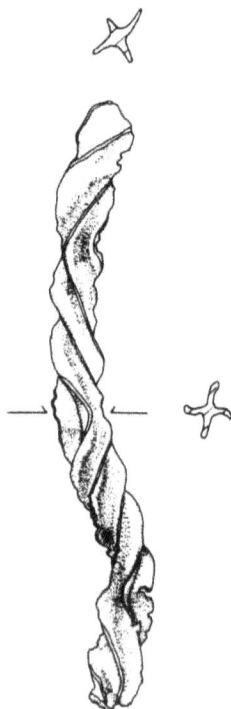

528

529

530

531

532

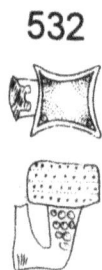

533
see
next
page

534

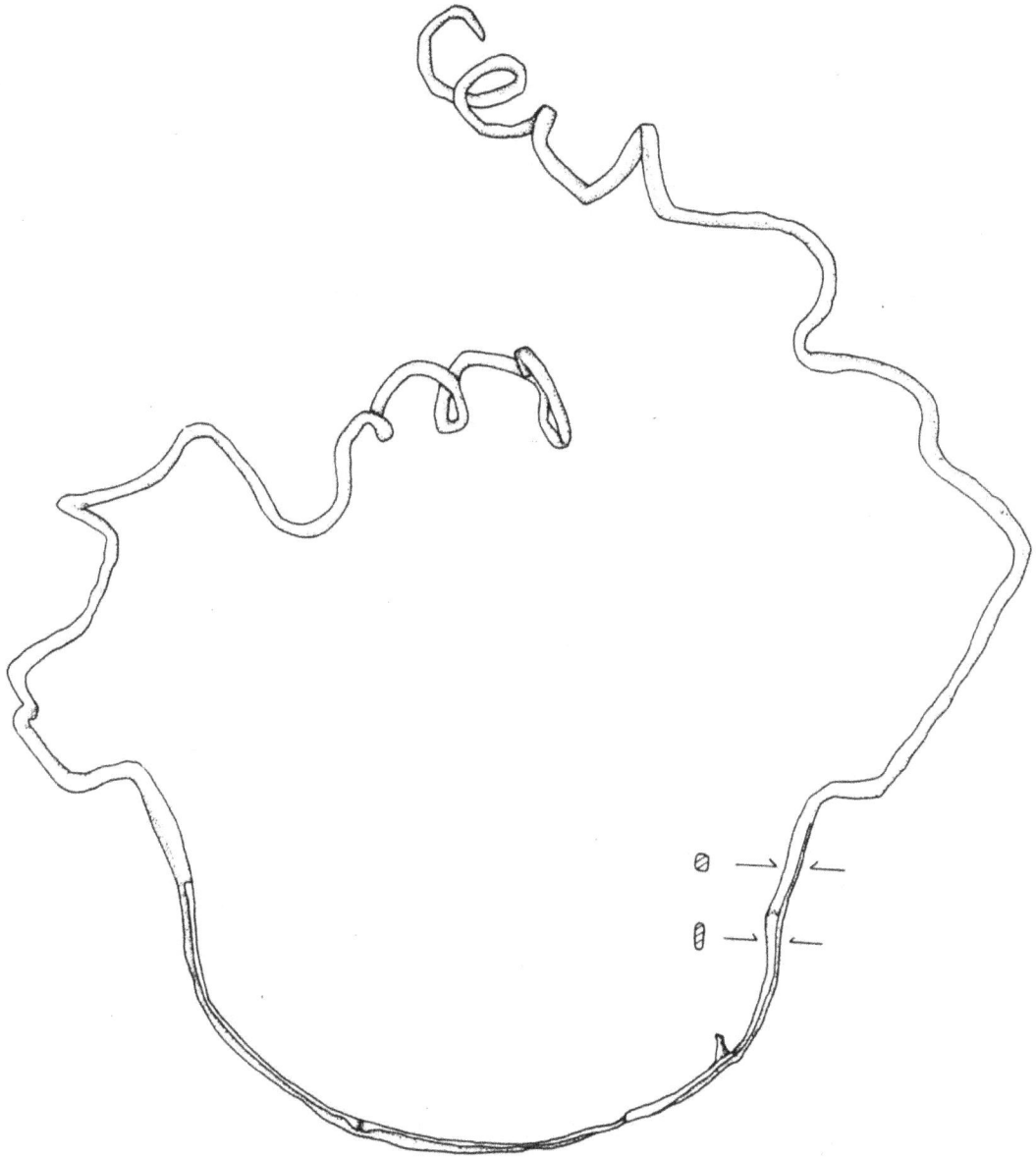

535

537

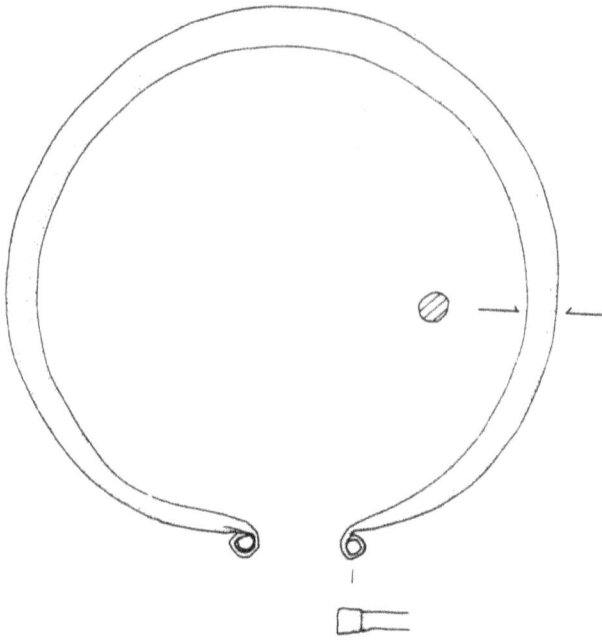

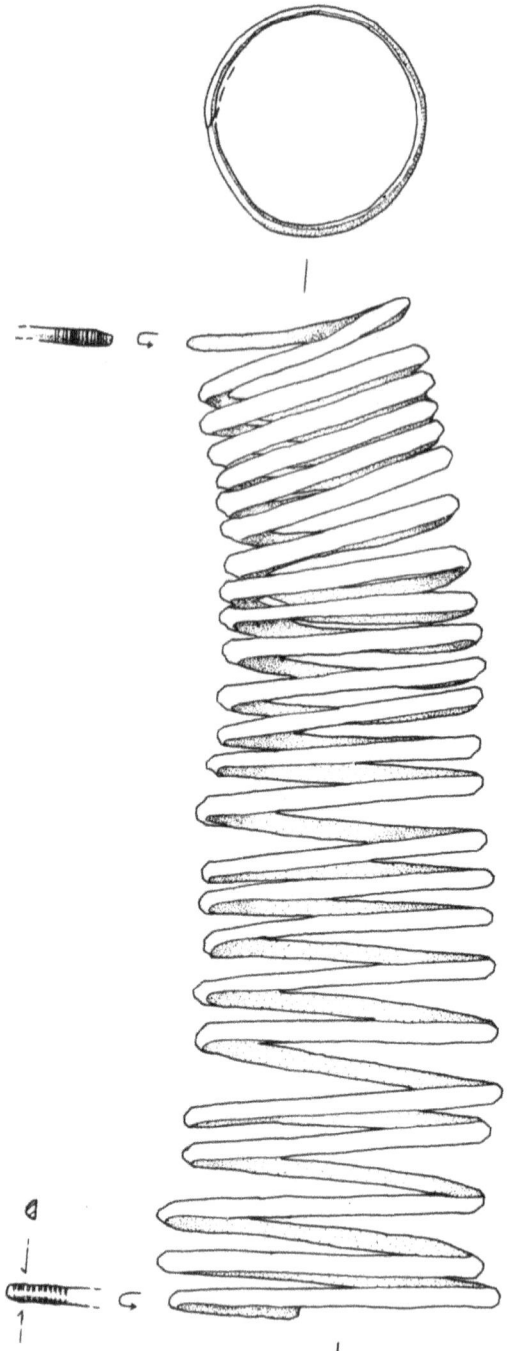

536

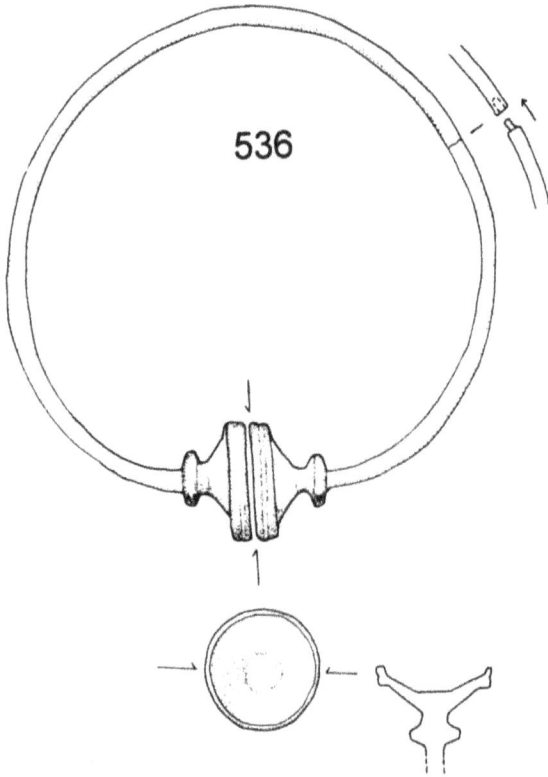

538

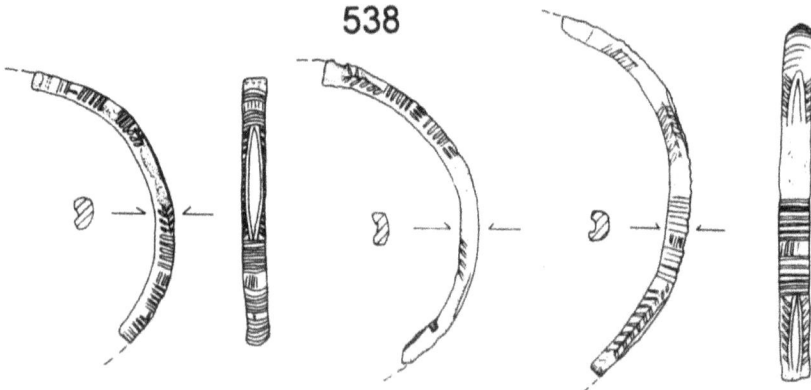

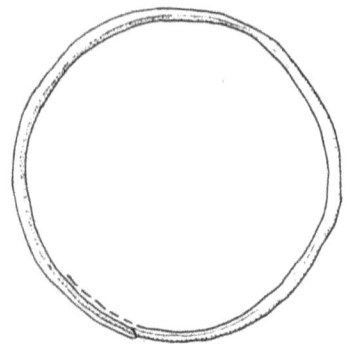

540

541

542

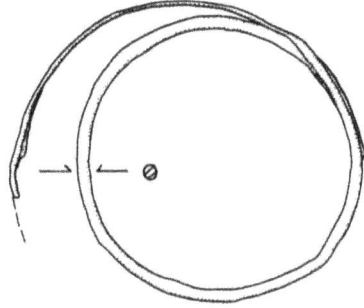

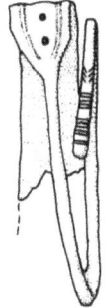

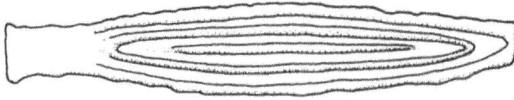

543

544

545

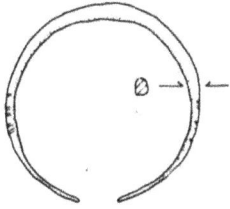

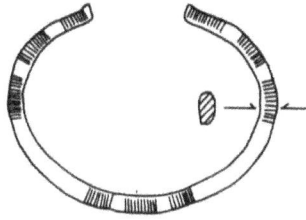

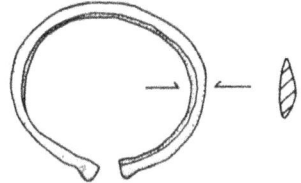

546

547

548

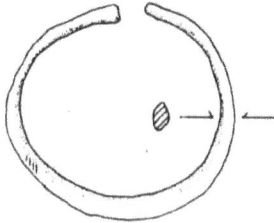

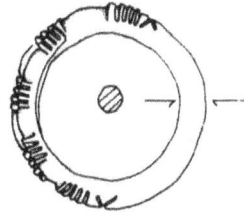

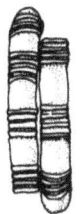

549

551

552

553

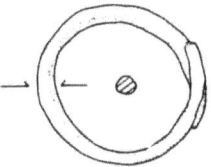

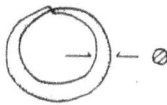

550

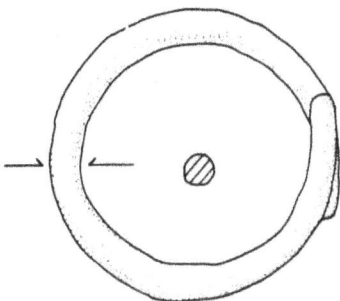

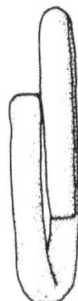

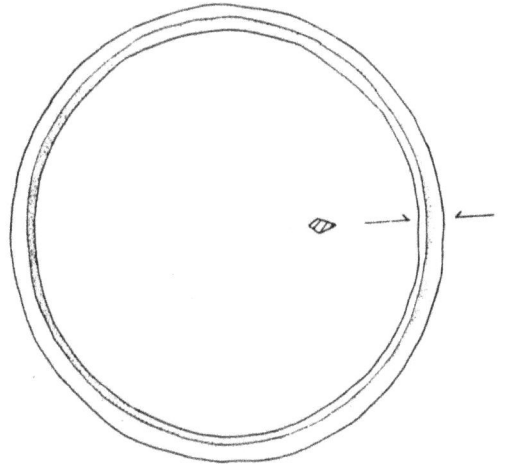

PLATES

Plate I

97

98

Plate II

99

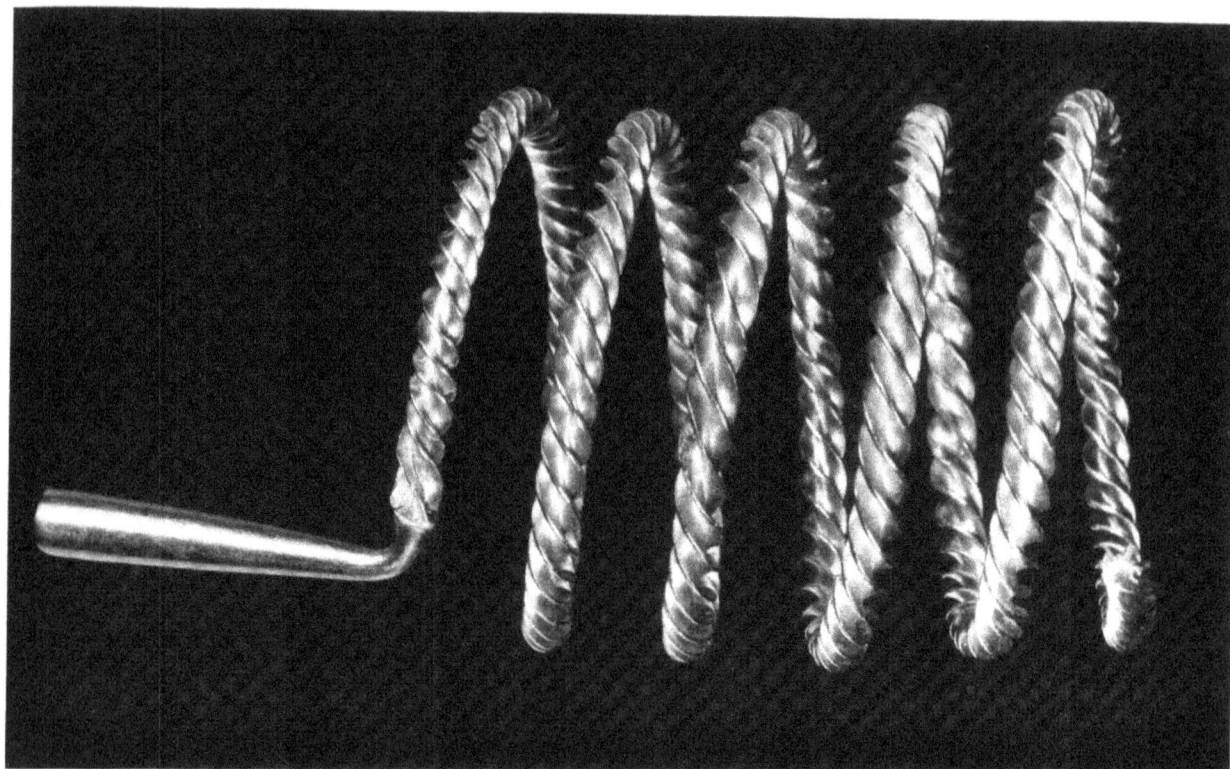

Plate III

100

101

102

103

104

Plate IV

139

140

Plate V

527

www.ingramcontent.com/pod-product-compliance
Lightning Source LLC
Chambersburg PA
CBHW061301270326
41932CB00029B/3422